Jim McDonald worked for forty years as a professional biologist and ecologist. During that time (and longer) he has been an ardent rod fisher of Atlantic salmon, trout and sea trout. He combines his interests in environmental issues and fishing with those of writing. He now urges an honesty and realism in how we approach matters of conservation, as opposed to following any assumed norms of popular and political correctness.

To Les, Dennis, Vic and Doug, for all you have given me and for being there when it mattered most.

"… This is, I believe, a profitable, accurate and comforting point of view that, among other things, makes you want to spend a lot of time fishing, not as Robert Travor pointed out, because it's so important, but because everything else we do is equally unimportant." (John Gierach – *Even Brook Trout Get the Blues*)

"And besides fishing there was reading. I've exaggerated if I've given the impression that fishing was the only thing I cared about. Fishing certainly came first, but reading was a good second." (George Orwell – *Coming Up for Air*)

Jim McDonald

RIPPING THE VEIL

Reflections on the Life of a Rod Fisherman

AUSTIN MACAULEY PUBLISHERS™

LONDON • CAMBRIDGE • NEW YORK • SHARJAH

A CIP catalogue record for this title is available from the British Library.

ISBN 9781528917926 (Paperback)
ISBN 9781528917933 (Hardback)
ISBN 9781528962117 (ePub e-book)

www.austinmacauley.com

First Published 2022
Austin Macauley Publishers Ltd ®
1 Canada Square
Canary Wharf
London
E14 5AA

This book would not have been written but for the experience of a lifetime in meeting other fishermen on the riverbanks and lochsides of Scotland. Those whom I have met are too numerous to mention, although many are identified in the pages of this book. Thank you to all of you for the times we have shared.

Thanks to AM Publishers for agreeing to publish this work. An especial thanks to Adam Lake, Publishing Coordinator at AM for bringing the work to fruition.

Finally, an extra big thanks to Catriona, my family and friends who have all tolerated my enthusiasm for fishing, over the years. Your patience in listening to tales of fish caught and lost (mostly), as well as endless pictures of my catches through the ages, is much appreciated!

Table of Contents

Foreword

Most of this book was written in 2015–2016 with subsequent further notes and musings. In the Introduction, I make some quite bold assertions regarding my attitude to fishing, not least my disquiet about the prevalence of catch-and-release policy and how this has affected my engagement in spring-salmon fishing. My position regarding spring fishing has changed somewhat over the years, although not my underlying disquiet over the policy. I have let the Introduction stand as testimony to how I was thinking at the time of writing but have addressed the reasons for my changing position in the final chapter.

The east-coast salmon fisheries in Scotland have suffered massive losses in rod-caught catches in the past few seasons, so the underlying concern that I express throughout these pages has only deepened. This book was intended to share warm sentiments of the Scottish scene with like-minded friends and fishers but, regrettably, it may have become more of a somewhat reflective account of how things once were. I can only hope for an improvement and, in the final chapter, have stated my opinion on the importance of the angling body to the conservation of the Atlantic salmon. In this regard, I have grave misgivings regarding the recent categorisation of Scottish rivers and its heavy-handed and often irrational policy on catch and release. Anything that discourages angling effort is arguably detrimental to the ecosystem of which the Atlantic salmon is part.

Fishing has a great deal to do with solitude but it is also a cradle in which deep friendships are nurtured. During my life as a salmon fisher, my friend Dennis was a cherished companion. This is reflected in the dedication of this book to him and others. Sadly, Dennis has passed away. I have lost a dear friend and this book is further dedicated very much to his memory.

Laurencekirk, November 2019

Introduction

I cannot remember not being a fisherman but I do remember when I first caught a fish. It was not a big fish, not even a small big fish. It was not even a big small fish! But what a fish! Did I ever catch a better fish? Possibly not, although what on earth is meant by a 'good' or 'better' fish? Was there ever a fish of more importance? For me, of course not! The occasion was all important and seminal. This was when the subtle veil between air and water was ripped, when the very barrier between the banks on which I crawled and the foreboding depths of an unseen world were banished. And that, my friend, is what fishing is all about: The dipping into another realm; bringing to the light of day, creatures of unimaginable beauty from a watery world, things silver and gold, shining and resplendent.

But my fishing is more than a curiosity. It is a compulsion of uncompromising urgency to hunt and to succeed. How else can I explain a recent outing in pursuit of salmon that involved a round-day trip of ten hours motoring, horrendous midge infestation and the loss of three salmon, only to be followed two weeks later by a repeat trip of equal depravity and the loss of five salmon? (I shall, of course, repeat the venture with renewed conviction this coming season!) Or how indeed can I explain my insistence on one last further dripping cold drift in pursuit of trout down the far-side of a favourite Highland loch? Even the most empathetic of my companions found the depth of my compulsion bemusing, or so he said! And, at the end of it all, mine the glorious jurisdiction over what to retain and what to return, to accept or to decline, to catch or to release.

At this juncture, because I apparently condone the at least occasional killing of fish, I shall have lost part (indeed, perhaps most) of my readership. As far as I am concerned, unease associated with the killing of fish reflects the day and age in which I live. It reflects an era of indulgent political correctness of my peers who practice a popular if, to my mind, irrational conservation of sorts. They fish but they do not kill fish. Indeed, for much of the time they fish and cannot, by decree, kill fish. Please do not get me wrong. We must all decide on issues of behaviour and I have no problem or bone of contention with those who hold a very different point of view from my own. I have many dear friends who brave the cold of a Scottish spring to catch and release the early salmon. Some fish all season with this ethic. I have a sneaking, if somewhat uneasy respect for their efforts but I do not share their enthusiasm. They have learnt (almost!) to leave me alone and, mostly, I leave them alone with regard to spring fishing. They are my friends and I respect their decision. They struggle to sustain something that has been important to them and the Scottish tradition. However, we live in an age of inherited and often borrowed luxury, one of easy conceit born of complacent, comprehensive ignorance and arrogance. It is the age of popular, righteous and, crucially, much publicised and often cynical bandwagons. It is the age when, to keep fish, is considered by many as being sacrilege. I do not buy into this attitude. I am not part of it. I cannot be part of it. Where I cannot choose to keep fish, I mostly do not fish. Indeed, if the motive for the now assumed correctness of catch-and-release policy is the conservation of dwindling stocks of fish, then I would rather not fish at all than to play this dubious game. For the most part, I practice what I preach: There are many rivers where you will no longer find me, at least for part of the season.

So, this is my philosophy on the beauty of fish and fishing: I am a naturalist but I am part of nature. I am a compulsive hunter but not a butcher. I am a killer but not a sadist. I am a realist and pragmatist, not an idealist or theorist. If I catch a fish, it is mine. I have sought and found it by entering another world. I have deceived it. I have got the better of it. I have done something fundamental to my nature and that of my fish. And I shall decide over its fate. It is now a matter between me and my prey. No one else is involved. No other opinion is sought or necessary. The moment is intimate and unannounced. It is not legislated. And very often, the fish will be returned. So, how do I decide on the fate of my captive? What, in that critical moment swings the balance between life and death? Is it a matter of type of fish and size? Is it a matter of hunger or compassion? Is it a matter of beauty or pride? Do I need a trophy to convince the sceptical? Perhaps it is all these things. Do I need answers to these questions? Do I care that I cannot understand my actions, that I cannot answer my questions? Do I worry about the perception of others? The answer: most definitely no.

And at this juncture, I may very well have lost most of what remained of my readership. And does this matter? Not to me, although it may be of some concern to my publisher! But the great thing is that I can now get on with the real job in hand without compromise. I can now share with the few who are left, the unutterable joy of ripping the veil that separates men from fish. I can in the most unapologetic manner describe what for me is the very essence of fishing. I can share the necessary intimacy of my contact with the hidden world and how I have responded to the occasion, not in a measured way but in the spontaneous climactic contact of two living beings where, on some occasions I, as hunter, have come out on top and have played god, in deciding the fate of another most beautiful creature. Of course, normally this is not the outcome and I am left disconsolate as the veil is restored and the fish, which I failed to make my own, sinks easily into its watery world. And, at other times, I shall decide to return my captive to its watery world, once more restoring the veil.

So, for the few who remain – for the few for whom a priest and a bass bag are given accessories and for whom the killing of fish is an expectation but not a compulsion, for those for whom the discretion that results in fish released or abstention from fishing are the very easy companions of fish sometimes killed – I hope you find some joy in what follows. I hope that, on occasion, you find yourself by my side in the full expectation of me handing you a bending rod and taut line connecting air to water and men to fish, joining the complexity of our perceived world to one which is essentially unknown. For some, this very sharing of fish and men is compulsive and that is why I must write what follows. And it is why you will be compelled to read my thoughts, displaying a compulsive curiosity for sharing my experience in much the same way that you cannot but stop and stare through the veil in crossing bridges over even the most modest of streams.

This book is not about the technicalities of how to catch fish. There are others much better suited than I to inform on tackle and methods. Indeed, the angling press continues to abound with such information. It does however have a great deal to do with the joy of fishing and the enthusiasm and compulsion that leads fishers to the waterside. For many, the pursuit of fish becomes a way of life and the very essence of this has been captured by a great many authors in the past. Their writings – often humorous and philosophical at the same time – embrace not only stories of fish caught (and often failure to catch fish) but also the myriad things that contribute to the whole experience. They often capture poignantly the emotions relating to landscape, waterscape and – not least – companionship amongst anglers.

I doubt if any other pursuit has such a wide and excellent literature as that associated with rod fishing. Occasionally, methodology and romance – the feeling for the whole business – are combined as in the writings of WB Currie (*Every Boy's Game Fishing*; *Days and Nights of Game Fishing* and *The River Within*). Bill Currie was important to my development as a rod fisher and I often return to his writing, not so much to learn something new but to smile in appreciation of a man who affected my life. The same is surely true of TC Kingsmill Moore (*A Man May Fish*) and Sidney Spencer, a fine selection of whose writings (*Fishing the Wilder Shores*) has been compiled by Jeremy Lucas. Some authors are just wonderfully entertaining – real wordsmiths; Bernard Venables (*The Gentle Art of Angling*) and, more recently, Brian Clarke (*On Fishing*) being amongst the finest. And then, there are the fishers who travelled, correspondents and diplomats such as Negley Farson (*Going Fishing*) and Robert Bruce Lockhart (*My Rod My Comfort*). These are the men who defied imprisonment (or worse) as they ventured forth with rod in hand in some far-off place. The fisherman's year described by Roderick Haig-Brown in *A River Never Sleeps* makes compulsive and wonderful reading. More recently, the wonderfully evocative accounts by authors such as David Adams Richards (*Lines on the Water*), Thomas McGuane (*The Longest Silence*) and a wonderful compilation of writings by John Gierach (*Death, Taxes and Leaky Waders*) maintain the tradition of literary excellence in expressing the essence of fishing. There are many more across the world and my hope is that you will find them. It is very much in the shadow of such greats that I find myself, with no great expectation that I can attain the heights achieved by such writers. I do hope however, that you will be sufficiently enthused by what I say, that a small nudge will push you from the shadows of my writing into the bright place shared by those authors for whom fishing is so much more than the mere catching of fish. If that be the case, then I shall be well-pleased.

A Child of the Firth

The joy of fishing has got an awful lot to do with anticipation and selective memory. Occasionally, something happens in the present (a fish might even be caught!) but, in the main, high anticipation and fond memory win through. They are more reliable companions to the whole angling effort than is the often-mixed experience of the actual, unedited event. How often is the blinkered enthusiasm for the outing marred by the frustration of what in fact happened? How many eagerly awaited trips to the water have been blighted by weather? How many evenings to the pool have been thwarted by biting midges or mosquitoes? And yet, what do we remember? Not the raging discoloured torrent of the afternoon or the maddening midge assault that made us run for high ground. No, we choose to remember the morning grilse caught or lost (lost fish are very important) before the flood. We choose to remember the sea trout netted before the midges did their worst. It is surely this selectivity of memory that fires us for the next round. It can keep us going even during the one trip. How else to explain that one final drift despite the cold, dripping-wet reality of the disappointing day, the one final cast when no other fish has been caught all day? So, we must conclude that anticipation and memory are integral to the fisherman's joy. With that in mind, they are surely things to be cherished and nurtured. They are of course the things shared – the spoken word – by countless fishermen as they meet and chat by the water or in fishing huts and pubs throughout the land. But there is a place for the written word that thrills in its naive enthusiasm and selective narrative of small triumphs, whilst buffering the reader from what would otherwise be countless volumes on frustration and disappointment. In what follows, I have cast a selfish line in search of what I am and why I fish. Perhaps, as I explore my own relationship to angling, others may find something of themselves and a shared joy in the realisation of what makes them fishers.

My early worldview was simple: in the beginning, there were shore crabs. Then there were eels. And then, there were other fish. I could end this chapter and, indeed, the whole book here and not too much damage would have been done. In doing so, I would have reflected briefly (but accurately) on my early years. I would have documented, if somewhat summarily, my history as a hunter. I would also have avoided the very real risk that, in trying to communicate further my enthusiasm as a fisherman, I inadvertently killed the joy on which I often subconsciously rest. This latter point worries me. There is a very real chance that, in expressing my thoughts, the bubble of excitement may burst and much of what I have subtly cherished and kept from the cold light of day may quite suddenly seem disappointingly dull and unimportant. How then would I be sustained through the periods of drought (both literal and metaphorical)? How would such dull images compare with the archive of jewels that are currently mine? Would I ever return to the water? Would casting a line seem utterly meaningless? I have faced this dilemma previously. It is many years since I first submitted a short piece of writing to the angling press depicting the capture of wild trout, a capture that proved to be a milestone in my fishing career. At the time of writing, the images were clear at the outset and, thankfully, they remained largely so at the end of my piece. Were they in any way distorted and tarnished by the effort of communication? Perhaps they were but time has proved a great healer. I now feel ready to revisit that very same occasion (among many others) with enthusiasm and joy, in the hope of sharing something of its excitement. I do not think the image in question has been damaged irreparably in the process of expression and I shall boldly assume that this will hold true for all other events that may surface and land on these pages. This is no light assumption because these are the images that will surely sustain me in later years when I can no longer take to the waters. Whatever, I do not feel much leeway in this matter. As with fishing, writing has become compulsive and, as with fishing, I cannot reason why.

I do remember some things before green shore crabs but they do not seem to have much bearing on the compulsion of fishing. These seminal memories are very vague. They seem to be mere snapshots and very grainy ones at that. In fact, the camera of my very early mind must have been well and truly out of focus and held at an alarming tilt, denying anything resembling reasonable perspective and appreciation. Is this normal? I assume so. I suppose the snapshots do form some sort of continuum, some sort of macabre and unfortunate cinema where proportion is discarded. When very young, I knew my childhood home to be mysterious and palatial. Years later, when revisited, it did of course seem quite modest and its grounds seemed quite small. But appreciation during those early years had a very different and, at the time, quite valid perspective. The darkness of one room harboured green goblins and fear but most rooms were realms of light and sanctuary. Trees in the garden were enormous and secretive but there were faces in their branches. These moved in the wind, sometimes laughing, sometimes scowling. This early continuum is more than visual. It is a world where sense of smell, touch and sound are also important. It goes far beyond the world of normal cinema. On reflection, all this belonged to a surreal but somewhat shaky world, punctuated by frames of outstanding clarity and sensual complexity. Weirdly enough, it is in this primitive category of high sensory impact that fishy things emerge, crabs and eels and other silvery things.

I do not recollect when I first encountered a shore crab. But 'encounter' would be the word. There are elements of surprised aggression and defence when man stumbles upon an animal that is so different to self. Perhaps this is not so surprising given our embarrassing inability to readily accept even small differences amongst fellow men. What hope then for a rational response when we encounter beings so different from ourselves? Whatever, there is something fundamentally intuitive about our uneasy response to larger crustaceans that scuttle off waving fearsome looking claws when disturbed. We do not need to be told that these claws can inflict damage, although careless proximity to such armoured weaponry will reinforce the need for respect; the nip from a larger crab claw is a timely reminder to handle its owner with care! No doubt, there is something deeply significant in the evolution of man that we should share some relic fear of such animal defences.

I do remember early crabbing forays with my father. These were certainly weekend or holiday occasions because he was a school teacher and a busy one at that. Our house stood well above the shoreline and had the most marvellous views to the south across the firth. The house seemed large, foursquare and built of red sandstone. When we first moved in, the house was still in some disrepair following military occupancy during the Second World War. It had recently been divided into four apartments, all at this juncture occupied by staff who taught at the local school. This occupancy by the teaching profession was no chance occurrence, because the local council encouraged staffing at the school by offering accommodation in the big house. It was the most idyllic place, with beech woodland to the west and south-facing grazing slopes to the north. The rest of the village with its harbour lay to the east.

My father was no naturalist. He had been brought up as a city child but city life alone could surely not explain his lack of informed interest in the natural world. I can only assume that chance opportunity, that might otherwise have fired his curiosity for the natural world, had not come his way. It was not the case that he did not care about living creatures. I remember him to be a very good handler of animals large and small. Dogs and cats were at ease with him and he dealt kindly with all sorts of offerings that our cat brought home; sparrows, shrews and mice were all carefully tended and given a new lease of life before leaving our house. He was also a fanatical gardener, with an emphasis on fine order. His lawns and flowerbeds were of the manicured type and I retain some treasured memories of the quite immaculate fruits of his efforts. But these memories are also indicative of my father's attitude and his relationship with nature. For him, a garden was a place of sustained order. He would strive to keep his borders free of weeds. His lawns would be mown with the utmost regularity and their edges trimmed perfectly. His plants were all exotics and hybrids, where shrubs and rose cultivars abounded. His efforts were greatly admired by many and his gardens were, indeed, truly things of beauty.

Over the years, I grew to appreciate my father's efforts to have been those of fighting against, rather than accommodating nature. Gardens are, after all, very often attempts at derailing the natural processes of plant succession. This does not mean that my father's efforts were misguided or unsuccessful. On the contrary, they resulted in some stunningly beautiful creations. However, in achieving fine simplicity, my father's gardens lacked complexity. I do not recall there being many bird nests in his trees and bushes. Perhaps the branches were too carefully pruned to provide the necessary combination of cover and perches. Nor were there lots of butterflies. Boggy ground was something undesirable and something to be drained, rather than something to be welcomed and conserved. I do not recall nettle patches as being welcome; they too, along with many other 'weeds', were eradicated. Such constant battle for clean simplicity can result in beautiful effects but it does no real favour to other components of our natural world.

Where my father lacked exposure to the natural world, he provided it for me in his choice of early career. As a very young child, I grew up surrounded by sea, woodland and grassland. Wild flowers abounded, seabirds and songbirds were ever present. Owls hooted at night, wild cats were spotted and, on the shore, crabs and eels abounded.

We would take to the seashore, father and I, at low tide (sometimes very low tide). Father would be dressed for the event, wearing his old army mackintosh (heavy duty), boots and gaiters. The picture would not be complete without his pipe and accessories. The latter took the form of tobacco pouch stuffed with Balkan Sobranie or shredded St Bruno (the shredding being a positive industry in its own right) and a box of Swan Vestas, Bluebell or Vulcan matches. Cleaners and spills remained at home. They were the things of evening activity when father would sit by the hearth in his own private cloud of smoke and make careful comment in purple Faber crayon in the foolscap jotters of his pupils. The final accessory for crabbing – and the only one that was essential – was a large zinc pail. It was into this that the catch would be placed.

And what a catch it was! Father would lead the way, heading for the low tide mark and pulling the swathes of bladder wrack from dripping, barnacled boulders as if he was drawing the curtains from the stage of seashore life! And that is exactly what he was doing, because there, in front of his young enthralled audience would be one or more – sometimes many more – of the menacing green-armoured brigade. If it was opera, it was Wagnerian on the grand scale! These were intensely exciting moments of great enthusiasm laced with awe as the larger specimens tinged with orange were uncovered. It was always the quest for these leviathans that kept us at it and they were always near the low-water mark. So, time was tight. We had to keep at it or the opportunity would be missed. For me, the sense of disappointment and of time lost was great if we missed our chance. The day was over and nothing would be possible until the following, when we would time our assault with more precision. (I must have been too young to be let loose at strange hours because, for me, these early years held only one tide per day.) This sense of urgency and the need for opportunism is something that persists. It belongs to the hunter and makes me fanatical. How frustrating it still is to arrive at some river and find it dirty and rising and the fishing off. There is always some kind soul who will show me his gleaming catch taken just before my arrival and before the river became a dirty waste channel. I am sure father was much more philosophical and measured in his approach; there would always be another day. But, for his son, this was doubtful consolation. It required a strong diversion for me to feel anything other than pressing impatience. Such is the lot – and, no doubt, the mark – of the fanatic.

And into the pail would go the catch. This must have been the birth of me the collector. I had a similar passion for wild flowers. They would be picked in abundance, sweet red campion and stunning sky-blue forget-me-not mixed with yellow buttercups and yellow-white daisies. They stood in jars of tainted water, often on some dull shaded shelf in the lobby, only to wilt rapidly, then die and decay. Occasionally, some specimens would make it to blotting paper and careful insertion between the pages of *Encyclopedia Britannica*, only to be forgotten and retrieved by some chance enquiry in later years. The common denominator was that of collect and die. If the life of local crabs was better off than that of local flora, then it can only have been marginally so. Father and I would fill a pail (or two) with scuttling members of the green hoard. This, as with the collecting of wild flowers, was a compulsive activity. Nobody blew a whistle on when to stop. Generally, the approaching tide would draw a halt to the mayhem and the catch would be admired; green and orange protagonists, waving angry claws in our direction. And, having amassed the day's treasure, we would tip the buckets into the push of some flooding rocky pool amid the weedy slipperiness and watch as the scattering multitude waved in defensive retreat. (Here, I was practising catch and release but, of course, shore crabs were not for eating.) Rapidly, they dispersed and took refuge behind weed and rock in some transient haven. We would return! Why on earth did we do this? What compelled us to hoard these creatures, as we ignorantly grabbed them from hard-fought territory? Our efforts must have represented the most thorough of evictions and destruction of social order in the crab world and yet we did not think in those terms. We wanted to touch them, to keep them, to show them. It was a necessary ritual where merely knowing that crabs lurked under weed and stone was insufficient. We had to remove them – albeit temporarily – from their hidden world and behold them as things caught, trophies of our curiosity.

There was a phase where my need to hoard and cherish reached the sublime and the ridiculous, at the same time. Our proximity to the seashore meant that I could replenish tanks of seawater at will. It was hard work! Down to the shore and back with as much salty water as my small frame could lift. I had learnt the hard way (harder still, for the crabs involved) that failure to replenish the tank on a regular basis would result in a stinking soup of dead crab, once smelled, something to be avoided! Hard grind aside, there was no impediment to my daily sorties to the beach. This was the grand age of freedom before the onset of dreaded formal schooling. The days were mine to fill with hoarder's glee! I would not be stopped. My tanks were improvised and devoid of all features that might have been of interest to their unfortunate inmates. No luxuries of stone and weed, here! These tanks were biscuit boxes in the raw – fine metal constructions bearing the proud logo of Macfarlane-Laing, the biscuit makers for whom my grandfather worked. The tins stood proudly on the flagstones in the shade of our house door with chicken-net topping that restrained the unfortunates. It would have been a tough call for any crab to climb the slippery walls on the road to freedom but I was taking no chances – hence the chicken nets! I cannot remember how long this persisted but I do not think it was a winter activity. It may only have been a matter of a few weeks. I regret I may have induced cannibalism amongst the hoard. (How often must a crab eat?) What I do recall very clearly is the day of mass escape. It did not have a happy ending for either crabs or me. On looking at the carnage, it took my young mind a few minutes to comprehend what had befallen my captives. The neat order of my tanks was in disarray. The wire toppings were cast awry and, of the sorry inmates, there was little sign. However, a trail of visceral remains made a crude vector of destruction. Broken claws and smashed shells spoke of a gruesome and chilling end. The culprits were the haughty gulls that wheeled in noisome throng around the battlefield, swooping on what small vestiges of life as could be found. A sorry sight indeed!

I do not recall a renewed effort on my part at caging animals. It was my first acquaintance with death (certainly mass death) and it was a far from happy experience. I did not fully understand (or acknowledge) the reality of what had happened but I was aware that my actions had, in some sorry way, resulted in the eventual demise of what I had cherished. Perhaps, not surprisingly, my enthusiasm for collection of most things living waned and, from that fateful day, crabs and flowers remained untouched. Bird nests were never explored or raided. Butterflies and other creepy-crawlies were safe. I progressed from compulsive and naive collector to selective hunter and observer. I began to need some primitive rationale to the pursuit of nature. This was not a particularly conscious decision on my part. It was more a sense of place in the wider scheme of things, a sense of place that has persisted to this day.

Gradually, my focus on things fishy and how to catch them became sharper. However, there was a middle stage – a refinement of crabbing – that still involved my hands and knees (and feet) and that had nothing to do with rods, lines and hooks. The lawns of our garden sloped steeply to the south where the waters of the firth were met by stony shores. It was here at the upper tide limit where fresh water trickled through the stones that small eels gathered. No doubt, there was seasonality attached to this occurrence but, for me, there were no breaks to the endless exploration of the shore. The stones hid eels and they were there to be found, sometimes in abundance, sometimes less so. The water itself was only seepage. I recall an old drinking trough by the roadside that would freeze in a hard winter but its usual overflow contributed to the fresh wetness. It is still there. The trickle could never be called a burn. Even the label of ditch would have been excessive but, what water there was, proved sufficient to attract the tiny, slippery elvers. Their fate was uncertain. They had certainly travelled from afar – although I did not know it at the time – but where would they go from here? Perhaps they would wend their way to the west until they encountered the big river and then continue upstream until they found some sanctuary for their adult life. Eels are truly remarkable creatures and I was to encounter them in more adult form on many subsequent forays with rod and line. But this was my introduction to their type and my curiosity was high. Inevitably, they became the object of my collector's instinct but I think they escaped the insult of confinement in homemade tanks. Eels collected and placed in small hand-moulded dams in the gravel were soon eels released as the tide approached its high mark and swept through the tiny, transient pools.

There was one other event that spurred my initiation and no doubt confirmed my fate. This was very much an occasion as opposed to an on-going process. As a family, we were not in the habit of travelling long distances. People generally did not travel far in those days. We did make a couple of massive pilgrimages to the south-west of Scotland to visit my grandparents on mother's side of the family. I recall one journey by train and one marathon drive by car. The latter took two whole days and involved three ferry crossings and an overnight stop. (Spean Bridge comes to mind – and my young eyes did see a large brownie jump in a nearby loch!) An exception to the rule of little travel was an outing by car to the west coast at Poolewe, where we were resident for a few nights at the local hotel. For those who know the place, you will appreciate that, in the 1950s, arriving at Poolewe was akin to arriving at Mecca – at least in the context of salmon and sea trout fishing. Things have changed and fish stocks are now much diminished but hanging in there! Two memories are paramount. Firstly, my elder sister and I were awarded the immense privilege of sounding the large brass gong that summoned residents from the far-and-wide recesses of the hotel to the dining room. This task was carried out with a great sense of excitement and urgency. Then, one day, I was cut dead in my tracks. The gong stick remained high and the gong remained silent. There, on a large silver platter before my eyes, was a gleaming bar of silver. I had never seen anything like it. The salmon – for that is what it was in all its new-caught glory – was a fanfare to all things piscatorial. It heralded the age of clear intention and addiction. I was utterly captivated, hook, line and sinker! I gazed at that fish for an interminable period. I could not eat. I left the dining table and stared at it. I returned to the table and sat down again but to no avail. I went back, unbelievingly, to the fish – and it was still there! It was real! I just could not keep my eyes off it! I had not a clue how you would go about catching such a fish but I knew it was special and, with mixed feelings of excitement and trepidation, I knew that, one day, I wanted to make such a capture for myself! How big was it? I have no idea because I had no frame of reference. The mind will always play tricks in such matters. It appeared very large and probably weighed double figures in pounds. But it hardly matters what it weighed. It was bigger than anything I had ever seen and it made a glorious impact on my young mind. I can see it yet and its glory has not diminished!

So, these were the formative years; the seminal events from which everything else flourished. I am sure my appreciation of light and my joy in painting grew from these early days. To this day, I can be stopped in my tracks by the brilliance of bold colour or subtle shade. It was years later that I first trekked in the Torridon hills and came quite suddenly upon the most stunning shine of bell heather in the early morning light. The deep purple-pink hue of one tiny clump was intense in its reflected light. It seemed to blossom on my childhood memories of glorious pink campion. Strangely, I remember that shock of colour more than any trout caught later that day. I still marvel at the pale ice-blue of forget-me-nots on the shingle verges of the Tay and they take me back to their close relatives growing in the banks of woodland where I roamed as a young innocent. The light on the firth was often stunning, both at dawn and early dusk. Red morning skies in winter vied with evening sunsets. They have since been equalled but not bettered by late November skies over the lakes in Sweden beside which I lived for many years. Their memory has been vindicated by stunning silhouettes of rock and tree on the banks of Craggie, nailed irregularly to a deep red banner to the far west of Sutherland. In the summer, the transmitted light from the setting sun set the red-brown sails of herring drifters alight as they navigated a safe haven to the west. No doubt, trawlers were under diesel power by this time but some sails were still set. The sentimental in me regrets their demise simply because some of the magic is lost from the transmitted light of the evening firth. And night skies were intense in their starlight. Years later, as I

24

lay cold one night in the heathery wastes of Cape Wrath, my gaze was transfixed by the awesome intensity of the deep boundless Milky Way and, for a few hours, the cold was unimportant and I became a child again.

Our family was to leave the Black Isle within five years of arrival. I have now told you where we lived and you can find the grand house for yourself if you find the water trough by the roadside. I know there was lingering regret about this departure on the part of my parents but perhaps that is always the case when big decisions are taken. Father was enormously over-worked as a teacher. He was conscientious and did not cut corners for the sake of expediency. Mother told me recently that, on his eventual departure, two posts were advertised where only one previously existed. Perhaps it took his departure to provoke common sense amongst the decision makers. Whatever, my father's letter of reference was strong and he was successful in his application for a promoted post to a city school. It was not all negative. I am sure the challenge was exciting for the whole family but I was aware of leaving something special. Professionally, father made a great success of his career. He became respected as a good teacher but also as a people's person. He made time for the individual and, for the many who knew him, he was an unsung hero in this regard. At his funeral, a city councillor introduced himself as being a pupil of father, from fifty years past. He wished to be there and share in the celebration of father's life, not because of what father taught him but because of what my father was, how he was with people. Wonderful!

But part of my father's legacy in having lived on the Black Isle was unplanned, unpredictable and unknown to him at the time. It was also much more intimate and subtle. He had somewhat inadvertently instilled in his son a sense of wonder and curiosity for things natural, an appreciation of form and colour, and for some unfathomable reason, an all-consuming desire to catch fish. It is only now that I realise that these writings are more about my father than myself. How strange that it should only now have become apparent.

Going Back

Leaving places and people you love is always hard. The more intense the love, the harder the departing will be. The sensible thing is not to return but to make the break clean and uncomplicated. But love is not always sensible and, the deeper the love, the more compulsive the return and the reunion with the loved one or the loved place. This is surely fateful and the expectation beyond the immediate joy of reunion is not necessarily one of happy outcome. It cannot have taken many months of new-found city life, before the decision was made for our family to return to the Black Isle for the month of August. The parameters were, of course, now different and probably ill-defined. As a family, we would return as visitors, people who had left and who would now return with a sense of belonging that was inevitably incomplete, both for us and for those whom we met. I am sure there would be nothing intentional in any reservation shown but I am also sure that any planned meeting, as was now the case, compared with the casual neighbourliness that we experienced when resident, promoted very different sorts of contact and appreciation. Whatever, we returned as holidaymakers with no doubt very different points of agenda. For my parents, there would be the meeting with acquaintances, the exchange of news and the subtle assessment of decisions made. It cannot all have been straightforward. Mother had lost her best friend Bette, from Black Isle days, to cancer, shortly after our departure south. It was a sad and disturbing day to share my mother's distress when the news came through that Bette had died. This was my first encounter with the open wound of grief in the passing of loved ones. So, the return was compromised. It was repeated the following year but, after that, the ties were laid aside and the attachment waned. I later learnt that, for my parents, the emotionally unsettling nature of these return visits outweighed any real joy of temporary re-acquaintance.

Of course, for me, the return agenda was very different from that of the rest of the family. Things had not happened on the fishy front during the months in

Edinburgh. That was not a source of disappointment or frustration because, what I had not known, I could not miss. But then, the intimated return to paradise awoke strange longings and expectation: The sweep of salty, wet weed as crabs scuttled in retreat; the shimmering elvers as wet stones were turned and the enthralling impact of having seen a caught salmon – the king of fish – in all his silver splendour! My agenda was fish and how to catch them. So, in this awareness of impending holiday, I experienced my first sense of eager anticipation based on distorted memory – surely the very essence of all good fishing trips!

Somewhere, in these early proceedings, a couple of hand-line frames, replete with lead sinkers, appeared. Father must have taken some initiative here, because I had no idea what they were on first sighting. However, for some reason that remains unclear, I decided to build a fishing rod. I have absolutely no recollection of having seen a rod in the flesh before this date. Nobody talked fishing; nobody showed me a rod. What I do remember is a cardboard jigsaw puzzle of an irresistible angling scene. The image was one of encroaching, sky-high banks in darkest browns and blue-blacks; an image of deep wooded canopies of orange-tinged branches and deep swathes of tea-brown, orange-flecked water, lighter over the shallow shingle and darker and more sinister towards the shady far bank where it swept out of sight. And to the fore, an angler – trout fisherman – plying his art with rod flexing in the cast, body angled to the action and creel draped from his shoulder. It was a picture with balance, where clever perspective heightened the anticipation of the moment. It was utterly captivating. I loved this jigsaw and used to stare at its completed image (one piece missing) time and again. I must assume that this and other fishy pictures introduced me to the reality of rods. My own prized creation was made from the stoutest possible of all garden canes, something acquired from a garden bundle, to be adorned with ring-eyed screws at regular intervals. It featured a handle made from coarse, rolled plastic bags, covered by two rubber grips. This primitive rod assembly was transported lovingly by my father on the roof rack of a very over-laden Morris Oxford. I, for one, was ready for the off. There may have been other paraphernalia (clothes, for example) that concerned my parents but, as far as I was concerned, further build up to departure was now time-wasted. The rod was ready – that was what mattered!

I seem to remember a very cheap, black-plastic, centre-pin reel appearing at some stage. This was acquired on arrival from the now-defunct store above the harbour on our return to the Black Isle. The reel did not have any form of ratchet, rendering it utterly useless in my eager but inexperienced hands. In practice, I recall a length of coarse line (borrowed, no doubt, from one of the hand-lines) tied to the top rod ring. At least, I had the option of holding my bait a few feet out from the harbour wall.

And harbour wall is where the action was. It rained heavily during our two August visits. I can remember one late morning of sunshine but I do not think there was much more. Perhaps that helped my parents decide on other venues for future holidays, although rain seemed to feature in most of these too! The big event took place as the rain slackened one early evening. I do not recall the immediate build-up but, by now, you will understand, it must have been intense. Father, as always (and most laudably), would be accommodating the interests of the whole family. The trip would only progress if my mother and two sisters were happily occupied with some other activity. Whatever, we eventually found ourselves in the lee of the stone building that adorned the innermost harbour wall. Father was kitted out in his usual garb of ex-army gear, dressed for all eventualities of the inclement kind. (Where on earth had he found space in the family car for all this stuff?) We were at the ready! The tide was nearly in and the gently swelling water pushed the limit of barnacle and weed cover on the sandstone haven. At some point, presumably earlier in the day, we had collected some whelks as bait. It was one of these unfortunate creatures, who, in prised and careless manner now adorned my hook. Neither father nor I had the slightest clue how to tackle up. There must have been a weight somewhere along the line (quite literally) and that must have been father's doing, likewise the choice of hook and bait and where exactly we should fish. So, there I was, in all eager anticipation, oblivious to the cold and wet, baited hook and rod to the ready. The bait was now in the water and by raising the tip of the rod, I could intermittently make out the light-coloured whelk, only to lower it once more into the welling depths. The tide was about six feet up the wall from its muddy bottom of stone and weed and it was into this depth that I stared.

And then it happened, the all-transcending moment that fishermen await, the strumming pull from a fish! It was so unexpected. It always is, even to this day! One moment, you are all-concentration, the next you are in contact with another world. You are pulled into it quite literally if you are off-guard with big fish in fast water! It is not that you do not expect the bite – in more recent years, I have even, on occasion, become confident about getting one – but the actual moment is always electric. It is the very essence of fishing. It is the moment when the veil is broken, ripped apart in tactile adversary. Years later, on the banks of the Tay, I would watch and marvel as my acquaintance Tommy fished for and hooked salmon on fly, spinner and worm. His thrill in contact was the equal of that experienced by all others on the bank. The thing is, Tommy was profoundly blind. Seeing fish take is great but the pull is what matters.

It would be fine to recount that this first fish was ceremonially removed from its watery place on to the rainy environs of the harbour wall but it was not to be. No sooner had the bite been made, the pull registered as a jigging taut line and a deep flash of silver seen, when all went dead. This was one of the dull moments of despondency that is the lot of all fishers, the moment when contact is lost and the veil is drawn once more; the moment when the line goes slack and the two worlds are, once more, far-removed. It happens often (at least to me) and it now seems rather fitting that, in what was to prove a tough apprenticeship with little supervision, I was introduced to the despondent, fast on the heels of the ecstatic. I have experienced it so many times since! It can happen on unexpected occasions – isolated events – but it can also happen in patches of disconcerting regularity. Sometimes, you think you know the reason why but, at others, you remain disconcertingly unsure. Was I too quick? Should I have let him turn more before tightening? Should I have let him run and hook himself? The answer could very well be yes to all these possibilities – but not always! Was I too slow? Had he spat out the bait before I tightened? Should I have struck on seeing the fish before feeling the pull? Perhaps all these possibilities come into play and, on occasion, some of them may even be true! With experience and improved technique, I have learned to reduce the losses, to strike late or early. But it does seem that any such assertion or dictate of confidence merely invites a new circumstance that leaves me surprised and thoughtful, wondering what exactly went wrong.

This harbour-wall account would not be complete without the glorious moment of triumph and it did happen just moments after the first fish was lost. I am sure I did not do anything different – at least not wittingly – but, when the next pull came (equally as thrilling as the first), I tightened and the fish was on! The ensuing battle must have lasted a full ten seconds – a period of enormous significance for both me and the fish. It involved throwing the rod to the ground and hand lining the struggling slither of silver from the harbour depths. It also involved my not falling into the harbour, no doubt the more pressing concern on father's part! It was the most wonderful moment! The fish, as you may have guessed, was a harbour saithe – a silver, shining coalie – that must have measured all of five inches and weighed half that figure in ounces. But I did not worry about its small size. It was, after all, the biggest and only fish I had caught! I was a fisherman! I could catch fish, that is what mattered! That evening, having climbed the harbour brae to display my trophy to mother and sisters, was certainly one of the happiest and most seminal of my life. I lay awake, long into the night, thrilled by the moment and impatient for the next day.

The next year's visit was preceded by another crucial and unexpected development in my embryonic life as a fisher. It was a moment of real and defining magic. I can remember clearly, waiting in great excitement, for the disembarking of my grandmother from the Belfast plane. Now, grandmother was a veritable institution in her own right. She has been departed many years but I gleaned small insights into the ways of this remarkable woman, normally from small asides that my mother conveyed. These utterances did not fail to surprise and they contributed to the many-faceted memory of a very dynamic woman. Here, is not the place to digress to any extent on the lady (she deserves a volume in her own right) but it is pertinent to say that she was a communicator and mediator of the highest order. She was one of nine siblings – two girls and seven boys. For whatever reason, it fell to Meg (as she was known to one and all) to communicate with her siblings far and wide. This involved the avid writing (in immaculate hand) of extensive letters and their sending, mostly to far-flung parts of Canada and the USA and, crucially, to Northern Ireland. The letter content would be one of factual account (mostly to do with pressing news within the sibling family) but it was liberally sprinkled with opinion and, where Meg saw fit – as was often the case, – strict admonition. There were few – including family, friends, foes and, indeed, politicians – who escaped her pen. Her writing was no light undertaking. Meg scrolled freely into the wee small hours, conveyor of news good and bad, opinions shared or divisive. What she did do, was keep a sibling family intact and, in my case, crucially, keep them informed of her daughter's family news.

Somewhere, along the line, Meg must have made passing reference to my growing addiction for all things fishy, not least when communicating with her brother Sandy in Ireland. Now, Sandy was an enigma. I had heard of him. I had even met him on one occasion. He had held positions of influence in India and latterly in Northern Ireland. He was an irascible and complex character. As a child, my mother dreaded his visits. When he visited her family home, she, as a child, would enquire of him as to when exactly he intended leaving! However, what Sandy lacked in diplomatic manner, he countered with warm-hearted generosity. It was following one of grandmother's visits to Sandy that I found myself part of the welcoming committee at Turnhouse (Edinburgh) Airport. I must have been primed to the effect that her arrival was significant and I was not to be disappointed. The lady in grey descended the gangway bearing gifts from afar and there was no mistaking the content of the elongated wrapping in worn brown canvass that made up her hand luggage.

From Sandy, I received the following: One split-cane, seven-foot spinning rod; one Ambidex fixed-spool spinning reel; one Moore's of Belfast fly reel; one lidded Wheatley fly box, replete with flies (Irish dressings) and, finally, one leather-bound cast wallet. All the smaller items had been packed and delivered to me in an old, dark brown, leather-clad box with a thin matching strap. I learnt later that this was a gas-mask box from the Second World War. Now, you must be of a certain mentality to understand my joy. In fact, you probably must share the addiction of things fishy to make any sense of it at all. I was ecstatic! I had no idea what to do with the stuff but I knew that, somehow, it would open the door to my further pursuit of fish. I was not wrong in this assumption but its realisation was to be a slow and unpredictable process. What Sandy had done with such generosity was to ply me with diverse tackle (a truly wonderful gesture) but what he could not supply, and what I desperately lacked, was instruction on its use. So, here I was with fishing goodies beyond my wildest dreams. I had seen nothing of this tackle before and I assumed it be unique. In fact, I was completely unaware that there were more fishers than the four of whom I knew: my benefactor Sandy; the anonymous (heroic) captor of the silver salmon at Poolewe; my man in the jigsaw and, of course, myself! Disillusionment on this presumption was a slow and piecemeal process.

Initial progress involved the careful removal of the rod from its case and the joining of the two worn pieces of cane at their brass ferules. I marvelled at its crimson-red bindings, evenly spaced along its much-used length. The brown corks were smooth and stained and I could only imagine the fish this rod had caught. The rod fired a great enthusiasm for experiment and, in the confines of my room, I went fishing! I would stand or sit or kneel on my bed with assembled rod and gently flex its length. I would imagine a deep welling sea and the catching of its inhabitants. The rain would lash in my seething dreams and the boat would pitch and roll, as rod and I sought cover on the eiderdown deck, trying not to hit the white-painted sky too often and with too much force. Sometimes, I would fix one of the reels between the brass ring housings of the cork handle and purposefully caw the reel handle against the weight of some unseen fish, marvelling at the smooth progress of the two-tone Ambidex or the evocative, irregular tired rasping of the old brass centre-pin. In my mind, this outfit could not be bettered and it screamed of fish caught – fish I had not seen. But this ignorance only heightened the mystery and excitement. Fights were strong and the outcome uncertain. Occasionally, on the crest of a rolling wave, the top agate-lined ring would tap the racing clouds and rod and I would crash to deck. Then I would return the prized possession to the safety of its bag, carefully tying knots in its cloth ties but only to reopen and marvel afresh at its mystery. The box of flies played little part in these playful sorties but the flies were much prized. I spent hours opening the hinged lids of each compartment and pouring over their contents; the gaudiness of an Alexandra or the subtle shades of Olive and Mayfly dressings – they were all there. Of course, at the time, I had not the slightest clue as to what they represented, what they were called or how they might be fished, how they might be attached to rod and reel or how, in some manner, in some river, loch or sea, they might catch fish.

So, there I was, returned to the Black Isle for a further foray but this time with a real rod and reel! But it is one thing having the equipment, quite another having the knowledge on how to use it. It was soon to dawn on me how inappropriate this gear was for catching fish from a harbour wall! Yet it had all been packed away and transported for the second trip. The rod and spinning reel did get one abortive airing but I shall return to that later. My clearest memories of this holiday have nothing to do with rods and reels but have mostly to do with hand lines. These memories do not relate to my own meagre achievements but pertain to another local addict who must have been a couple of years my elder. (There were now five fishermen in the world.) This lad was a veritable expert when it came to catching small saithe. I never saw him catch anything big but he positively slaughtered the harbour stock of tiddlers. He would stand at the extremity of the harbour wall, tight against the raised parapet and fished with urgency, as if his livelihood depended on it. You could see him from afar. He was always in place, easy to spot as I descended the harbour brae. Did he ever miss a tide? I doubt it! He was an ever-present of the harbour picture. His tackle was simple. It comprised a thin cotton line wound on a discarded wooden reel, the type of spool my mother had in her darning basket. At the end of this line, there must have been a small weight and hook but the action was so fast that these were hardly visible to my eye, which always focussed on his catch. He threw his baited line by hand and its thin length would travel a truly prodigious distance into the swell. It must have been all of ten yards. Occasionally, he would excel his usual performance and the small splash on entry would indicate a near personal best (perhaps twelve yards) further out in the firth. Then he would pause and his line would straighten and his bait sink and start to fish. He would feel for the bait by pulling gently on his line and – wonder of wonders – he would suddenly make contact! For him, the thrilling pull of a fish was a much-repeated event and this most surely resulted in an endless adrenalin rush. You could see his line jig and, in the depths below, another silver saithe would be seeking escape amidst the darting shoal. Up it would come from the green depths to be dispatched unceremoniously on the harbour paving, glistening beside its unfortunate brethren. And out the line would go again, each cast adding to the catch. This was fishing on the grand scale, where only the turn of tide would mark the end of play. The catch was always phenomenal in numbers and, but for its undiminished repetition on each successive tide, would have given rise to concern for the ocean's stock! What my acquaintance did with his catch remains a mystery; I can only assume that hunger was not a discomfort known to the village cats.

In later years, I was to reflect on this lad's phenomenal success with his chosen prey. His tackle could not have been more basic, his technique much simpler. He chose his spot well, other spots were not so productive. I would have loved to have a shot from his favoured stance facing the firth but it seemed sacrilege to suggest so. After all, he seemed to be a fixture as much as any stone in the harbour wall. Perhaps he could have been more generous in his attitude but I held no grudge towards him. I am sure his addiction was so severe that any interruption to the norm could have had quite alarming consequences! He showed me that, if you knew what you were about and were in the right place at the right time, you would catch fish, even if your tackle was, at best, primitive. It did not always have to be difficult. I learnt a great deal and my thanks are long-overdue to the young 'butcher' for his lessons.

As a postscript to this episode and before I leave harbour walls, I share one further memory. This relates to my earliest boat fishing. As usual, it had been raining all day and the assembled crew met on the wet harbour precinct. The paving was all dank and puddled and grey and the only concession to dullness was a hint of hazy lighting to the west. Even the boat was puddled and water had to be pumped and baled. It was an open craft with a powerful diesel engine and no doubt served its owner well in accessing some of the better local marks for coddling and flatties. The crew was four-fold and comprised our skipper who was a local banker, my father, the young saithe butcher and me. We did not venture far but headed past a rocky mark to the east of the harbour. For most of us, hand-lines were the order of the day but our skipper fished with rod and reel. It was not memorable from the amount caught. In fact, I am sure from our skipper's point of view, it must have been woeful. We did catch a couple of fish, a somewhat larger (but still not very big) coalie and a flounder. I say 'we' caught some fish. In fact, the coalie fell to our skipper and my father got the flattie. So I caught nothing and the butcher fared no better, despite practising his tried and trusted approach to harbour slaughter from the stern of the boat. What I learnt from this episode was that success from the shore does not necessarily equate with success from a boat – fishing does not necessarily improve with distance from the bank. Of course, there are great advantages to fishing from boats and some catches are utterly dependent on getting into deeper or more distant lies, be they in fresh or salt water. One evening shortly after our boat trip, I saw a returned fisher climb from his boat and walk from the harbour. His body pulled to one side and, from his straining hand, hung a plaice of marvellous proportions and size. Its huge red spots shone and glistened in the evening sun. It must have been very near the rod-caught record – it was truly massive – but it is extremely unlikely that such a fish could be caught from the shore. But sometimes the better fishing is in close vicinity to the shallows or the harbour wall, at least for some of the methods employed. It is also a matter of perspective and ambition. I am sure the young butcher got more pleasure from his success in the harbour than from his lack of success from the boat. The next day, he was back at his harbour post and normal service was resumed.

So, what of rod fishing? What, indeed! By the time of this trip, father had bought himself a spinning rod, fixed-spool reel, a few swivels, a couple of small blue and silver minnows and a couple of mackerel spinners. I recall his purchases in our local Edinburgh tackle shop. I assume that father described to the rather reserved shop staff what sort of fishing he might do or maybe the suggestion was put to him of light spinning from the shore. At any rate, father was now equipped with a functional seven-foot Milbro rod, a brand-new weapon cast in solid glass of very clean and light green hue. The reel was a black-coloured Intrepid model and the spool had been filled with seven-pound monofilament. I, of course had come prepared with cane rod and spinning reel – its spool half-full with whatever monofilament dear Sandy had last fished. This gear was no doubt all good and well for the catching of occasional mackerel and the like, if you knew what you were doing. But therein lay the problem: Neither father nor I had the faintest idea on how to proceed. Now, father may have had the opportunity to discuss the workings of a fixed spool reel with the shop staff – he may even have been shown its intricacies in some detail – but I assume not and, unless ignorance was pleaded, I doubt if the staff in question would have proffered much advice. They were a dour lot.

So, father and I arrived at Ness Point one calm and glistening evening, in glorious ignorance of what we were about but with rods in hand. Ness Point remains a captivating but deceptively dangerous place. It features a phenomenal current across the firth and its sandy beach to the east remains an alluring but most definitely dangerous place. To the west, shelves a shingle shore from which protrudes a small, barnacled stone pier that largely floods at high tide. We caught guppies on hand lines and improvised hooks here but I do not recall when. It is now more than sixty years since I first walked those shores. The sweep of shingle may be sculpted anew each winter but, essentially, things remain unchanged. It is still the place to spy dolphins and porpoises close at hand as they fish the tide race, at times incredibly close to the shore. I recall salmon showing in the current and often close to the tip of the sandy spit. Whether it was the sight of salmon from the shore or whether father had received some wisdom on the likely catch of sea trout or mackerel, I shall never know. It was the lure of salmon that excited me on our evening sortie. It was years later that I learnt that the rod capture of salmon from salt water was a most unlikely occurrence. At the time, our ignorance could not dampen our enthusiasm. So, tackle to the ready, we got stuck in. I have no idea what our expectations were, given that neither of us had seen a fixed-spool reel in use. All due credit to father because he had, at least, worked out that the line should come from behind the bale arm on its way to the bottom ring but here ended our expert knowledge. It must have been the inevitable tumble of loose line from an unchecked open spool that convinced father that bale arms should remain closed, including at the casting moment. It must also be noted that I offered no alternative strategy that might have alleviated the consequent problem. Our solution to getting the bait out was to slacken the slipping clutch to a minimum before casting. The accelerating bait then caused the spool to spin, releasing some line as the lure splashed a few yards from our wet and sandy boots. Now, if you have not seen a fixed-spool in use – as was our case – then a cast of a few yards soon defines the norm. Having cast, we then tightened the clutch and started to reel in the few yards of line that had been shot – assuming the sunk bait had not already snagged weed on the bottom while the clutch was being tightened. The whole experience was disappointing and frustrating to say the least. I was soon to work out what should be done but not on this trip. It was two somewhat bemused and disappointed fishers who left the beach that evening.

So, the second return trip was not a piscatorial breakthrough. At best, it marked the start of a tough apprenticeship that was to be based on trial and error and self-instruction. I desperately needed input from other fishers, although I did not appreciate this at the time. I had learnt some lessons but in the main my failings were unidentified and, therefore, unknown to myself. It would take other occasions and other events and circumstances before my stumbling career as a fisher could progress. I could still stare into the contents of my fly box from Sandy and realise that there were things to be learnt – things that would make me a better catcher of fish. At this stage, the flame was dim but, crucially, it still flickered. All that was needed was a bit more fuel and, slowly but surely, that was, indeed, supplied.

A Compulsion for Trout

When still a child and when still ignorant of most things piscatorial, trout fishing became important to me. It is difficult to see why this should have been so because I had not seen trout in the flesh and knew no one who fished for them, apart from the man in the jigsaw. However, somewhere along the line, I became addicted to the mystique of creels and rods and trout flies. No doubt, my early exposure to the picture of a trout fisherman with rod flexed against the dappled darkness of some steep-sided bank was important. Likewise, the allure of my Irish fishing inheritance from Sandy was no doubt seminal. Even now, I can close my eyes and still see the sombre but subtle shades of those Irish dressings, lough patterns that I should have cherished with more care, if only to preserve the link between Sandy and myself. The allure of flies was enhanced by the hours spent drooling over neat boxes of hooked creations from fur, feathers and tinsel, all on display under the glass counters of my local tackle shop. If the creations were fantastic to the eye, then the names were at least as evocative to the imagination. This was my introduction to Black Spiders, Blue Zulus, Wickham's and Watson's Fancies, Greenwell's Glory and Invicta, Coch-Y-Bondhu and Peter Ross. God forbid, the very names of these flies are sufficient to lure anglers, let alone trout! Whatever the reasons, my addiction to things 'trouty' developed early and has remained with undiminished enthusiasm, to this day. If my attention to trout has waned, it is only because I spend more time in pursuit of their larger, migratory brethren. However, a day on a wild-trout loch – and the trout must be wild – is till something that thrills in expectation and, at least sometimes, in execution. What I do know is that, if I should no longer fish for trout, I have sufficient wealth of memories and romance on which to reflect that I can dream contentedly and long, with just the necessary, thrilling anticipation of waters not yet fished to keen my imagination.

Having moved to city life, from the idyllic childhood nursery of the Black Isle, my opportunities for fishing became entirely dependent on the movements and holiday intentions of my parents. This was before I became aware of rivers such as the Water of Leith and the Braid Burn, both great streams but demanding of real skill if you are to get the best out of them – and real skill was something I most definitely lacked in those early years! I was also at a young age when I would hardly have been encouraged to venture forth alone on sorties to the neighbouring Border country, whose waters abounded with trout. That pleasure was to be delayed for a couple of years until pioneering trips on the SMT bus between Edinburgh and Stow were authorised. In the interim, my actual fishing time was, at best, sporadic but strangely compulsive. In retrospect, the remarkable thing is that, despite the few opportunities for catching trout and my complete ignorance in how to go about the business, my enthusiasm remained undiminished.

If you are a trout fisher, you will probably remember your first trout. I suppose that many – but hopefully not all – who fish today will have got started on stocked waters where big rainbows are released and subsequently caught without too much decrease in body weight. This latter comment, of course, presents a very jaundiced and prejudiced view of things and I must readily admit to the thrill of hooking and playing many of these monsters myself. However, I count myself lucky that my initiation to trout was very different and, for me, much more in accord with the very essence of trouting, namely in pursuing a quarry that belongs to its environment, a quarry that is essentially wild in nature and is often to be encountered in truly wild places. For me, there is something quintessentially antagonistic in catching trout that involves a measure of hardship. Perhaps there is something essentially Scottish in this assumption of pleasure in adversity. As a nation, we often seem to fare best when the going is tough and the wind is in our face. Maybe this attitude reflects the experience that opportunity afforded me. Whatever the reason, expectation was often greater than outcome in my early days of trouting. The wind was often quite literally in my face and my flimsy lines and casts would be knotted. If the wind proved favourable, there would always be tall grasses, trees, bushes or heather to ensure a glorious tangle. The sun would invariably shine bright and the water would be low and, if the wind dropped completely, then the midges and clegs would take over. On lowland waters, the fleeing retreat from death by a thousand bites was through nettles and brambles; on a highland water, it would be through slippery peat hags, outcrops of hard gneiss and deceptive sphagnum bog. So, why bother? Why not stick to something sensible and (perhaps) rational like stamp collecting?

The answer appears simple, although it probably emerges from a sea of complexity. For those who get involved (and I mean seriously involved), there are no alternatives. For the addict, it is far easier to go on than to stop and, for those who are truly smitten by trouting, we are talking serious addiction!

For me, the first joy of a trout on the bank was from the Uig burn in Skye. I count myself lucky to be a visual person, for whom most of life's highpoints have been defined by colour contrasts. Colour and pattern are so important to my appreciation of being alive, although other emotive stimuli are irreplaceable. Some descriptive writing is stunning. If you have not read Laurie Lee's *I can't stay Long*, then do so now! Good fishing literature has its highlights. I recently found *Fishing the Wilder Shores* – a selection of Sydney Spencer's writings edited by Jeremy Lucas – and what a fantastic read it is! Through his brilliant prose, Spencer invited me on board and I was soon pitching and rolling on previously unvisited and wild waters in the quest for salmon. I could even live the sudden pull and plunge as a heavy fish dived in the wave! Music is also intensely evocative and cannot be substituted. I find the piano music in the second movement of Mozart's Piano Concerto 21 and the second movement of Shostakovic's Second Piano Concerto to be profoundly moving. Others will share my delight in these works. Nature's music, including birdsong is near perfect to my ear and none more so than that of a blackbird or the lonesome piping of a solitary curlew in the still warmth of an early summer evening. And yet, without an awareness of colour and pattern my appreciation of this world would be very different. It was well into my adult life, that a bemused response to a chance remark led to my appreciation that not everybody identifies words with colours. When I read a word or say a word, I see colours – always the same pattern of colours for a particular word. I do not dwell on these colours but just take them for granted. Apparently, this is not a particularly uncommon phenomenon but, for those previously unaware of it, it can seem mighty strange. It has some interesting attributes. For example, a short word – such as the word *red* – is, for me, predominantly yellow! A lot seems to hinge on the vowel sounds but, whatever the details of brain pathways and the like, for those who experience synaesthesia – for that is what the phenomenon is called – the world of the word is a pretty colourful place. I suppose that, for those who share this mind-set, the world is effectively a pretty hallucinogenic space, without the need for extraneous chemical stimulation – lucky us! Apparently, for some people, sounds and smells can be felt, rough and smooth and the like. Words and colours are sufficient for me!

So, it is against this backdrop of colours and their importance to my appreciation of things that I remember my first trout. Now, to heighten the drama of the moment, I should say that 'trout' to my synesthetic experience is a very drab word indeed! It is essentially dullish grey with a tinge of air-force blue in the middle – not very exciting. You must now picture the scene of a watery-lit dampness of a west-highland evening in the month of August. The burn is running high, fining down after an earlier daytime spate. Its peaty colour is black, not yet the colour of tea water. Wads of aerated white foam are slowly skirting the edges of dark swirling pots, like dollops of whipped cream floating on stirred black coffee and the whole thing is singing as it races from pool to pool. An intense yellowness from the low evening sun is dappling the wet leafy banks and the still air is infused with aromatics from the vegetation.

Into this set, you must accommodate the presence of father and me, intrepid and ignorant anglers both. Father has concentrated mainly (and wisely) on the copious application of 'Flypel' because the midges are out but, somewhere along the line, we have managed to assemble a couple of rods. We are fishing worm, presumably because we had some vague idea (not entirely irrational) that catching burn trout on a worm could not be that far removed from catching saithe on baited hooks off a harbour wall. I recall flicking out a small length of line, pendulum-style, with a short length of hooked nylon as a trace. A couple of split shot, crimped to the trace, completed the outfit. How on earth we procured the worms, I have no idea – they were and always will be at a premium in peat lands – but worms we got and the burn trout loved them. If you have never fished worm for trout, then do it! Indeed, if you have never fished worm for salmon, get out there and give it a go – it is still legal on many waters! It is the most exciting tactile experience. First comes a knock, pause, knock and pause again, perhaps a double knock and then the glorious tightening into something unseen, tightening, pulling and surging – and often heavy – that makes the line sing! But you better be quick because it is surely only a matter of time before our 'masters' ban worm as they have prawn and shrimp for salmon in Scottish waters. God forbid that worm be banned for fishing burn trout but I am afraid that nothing now surprises me in our absurd quest for politically correct – but erroneous – compromise in things to do with conservation. Enough of that! At least I can still share the memory.

And now, I must transpose you – easily for those who have been there before – into the climactic moment, where dreams and imaginings become another sort of reality, the very moment when the veil is ripped between air and water, between man and fish. Because, into this glorious setting of watery light, I brought fish, trout caught, not by someone else but by me! And these were the most beautiful of creatures, quite defying my synaesthetic vision of dull grey and blue and quite dispelling that other misnomer of 'brown trout'. These were positive jewels of gleaming golden-olive flanks, with dark flecks and bright-red spots, contrasting with shining white belly and darker dorsal hues. They were not of course large – burn trout rarely are – but that did not matter. These fish shone in stark contrast to the dark water from which they had been removed. I am sure I got as much pleasure in communing with these gems as I would from any initiation to trouting that might have involved stocked fish that were ten times the size of these fingerlings. For me, this was the real thing and it still is. It is largely unfathomable why this should be so, why the catching of apparently wild fish should be so much more appealing than that of stocked fish. I have done both and there is no denying the thrill from heavy stock fish as they bend the rod. But smaller wild fish fight with disproportionate strength, reminiscent of the difference between the dynamic fight of wide-ranging mackerel compared with the steady, heavy pull of larger costal saithe or pollack. They can also be most gloriously coloured and are often of a lean but muscular form, expressing umpteen generations of evolutionary opportunity in a largely unchanged environment.

So, it was on the far shores of Skye – not so easily accessed as it is today – that I first caught trout. My start was faltering and chance-like and so was my progress for many years. I still had not met other trout fishers. I still ignorantly and naively assumed that the world of trouting was something into which I had strangely fallen, much as a fictitious alien in another universe. I assumed that all progress would be self-taught and my levels of ambition were for many years effectively undefined.

However, all was not lost and before leaving the stunning isle of Skye and its ancient volcanic rocks, let me tell you two other things – one of some inspirational import, the other merely bizarre. Both relate to events that took place on the one evening. We were fishing a pool on the Uig burn, father and I, not far from the sea. Again, the river was fining down after a spate. This time, we had company in the form of another not very experienced angler. Father and our new friend fished worm and – glory be – quite beyond our wildest expectation, our companion hooked a sea trout! Now this truly was something different, what with the determination of its captor not to release line and the innate ability of sea trout to display all sorts of aerobatics. The fight was short, hard and hectic but the line held and, after a couple of minutes, there on the bank was a two-pound bar of silver of a completely different calibre for us all to admire. I was duly awe-struck and quite uncertain as to how I would cope if, in the off-chance, I should inadvertently hook something larger than the norm. For some reason, I was fly fishing – my earliest recollection of such – and I have no idea why I should have done so. Whatever, I was most inexpertly casting a length of yellow and black twisted braid backing, a truly hellish surrogate for a proper fly line. Matters were not helped by using my one and only rod, the seven-foot spinning job from Ireland. I fished a single wet fly, an Irish dressing of a Golden Olive, possibly size ten. I did catch a fish and it did fight harder than anything I had previously hooked. I soon had an audience providing all sorts of impromptu advice on how to land my monster from the deep and, with or without help, soon had my prize on the bank – not a sea trout but an eel! I have never caught one on fly since and, although someone somewhere may well have documented such a catch, I have never heard word of it and my assertion of this strange capture is generally met with disbelief. It did happen!

Lack of opportunity meant that my progress was slow. I remember the following summer in Lochranza on the isle of Arran, fishing that deadly Golden Olive (God help me – an Irish lough dressing!) in a quite repetitive manner in the pursuit of small brownies in the local burn. I am sure there were sea trout to be had but they were well beyond my reach and expectation. My focus was on perfecting the catch of small but vigorous fish and they proved exceptionally obliging, generally thumping the fly as it swung on the dangle, moving from deeper water to the sandy shallows at the tail of the one pool I fished. If this was trout fishing, I was rapidly becoming expert, albeit under a very limited set of circumstances. I doubt if any of these fish weighed more than four ounces but I had found a way of catching them and my confidence grew out of such modest success. I soon expected to catch fish and their small size was not a matter of concern. In a strange and uncertain manner, I remained uncertain of my reaction should I hook something larger. I need not have worried for larger trout were not to come my way for some time. When they did, I felt ready for them, physically, technically and emotionally. I have no regrets over these slow beginnings. They reflected my transition from infant to young boy – from the capture of small fish to the hesitant expectation of things bigger – the expectation but uncertain assumption of my growing competence with rod and line.

It was in this sporadic and uninformed way that my fishing was to progress over the next couple of years. There were outings (not many) to the Gala water with father, where worms were inexpertly drowned in spate water at Stow. The same happened on the Moorfoot burn – a small tributary of the Gala – sometimes in spate but mostly in low summer water. These times were more suited to family picnics on hot grassy banks of the burn than fishing but, for a small boy, they still provided the opportunity for occasional success.

Two quite different but ultimately related sources of inspiration were to have a major and positive impact on my development. Both were unexpected and both had lasting effect. One morning, my father presented me, quite unannounced, with a signed copy of W.B. Currie's *Every Boys Game Fishing*. The inscription was dated and read 'Wishing you as much pleasure in your fishing as the author has had in his'. What a gift! The book is an uncomplicated mix of instruction and anecdote and I read it yet. For a young and inexpert enthusiast, it was to prove invaluable in nurturing improved technique but – and, in the long term, of equal importance – it fired the imagination of fishing in far places for trout, sea trout and salmon. What can match the evocative description of hill-loch fishing on the isle of Mull where summer sunsets provide the backdrop for dark hills silhouetted against a late evening sky? How thrilling is the description of how a great leviathan of a trout was moved to an improvised bait rig from the depths of a river in Lapland! The writings of Bill Currie have continued to inspire me but perhaps none more so than these early readings.

Currie got me started in earnest, perhaps not always as he might have intended and most definitely not always as I might have wished or expected! However, the overall progress, despite many bumpy moments, was in the right direction. It was the inspiration of his instruction and conviction that made me learn how to tie blood knots for joining lengths of nylon of near equal strength and the turle knot for tying nylon to hooks. What better way to present a fly? He taught me how to cast a line, how to keep the rod within a sector of loading on the back cast and delivery on the forward. He taught me the rudiments of watercraft, how trout face upstream and flee from the presence of stumbling and rod-waving anglers. He taught me much more. His writings were imbued with a sense of angling morality. He taught a respect for fish and other fishermen. There is a code of conduct, nothing restrictive but just a common sense of decency and generosity that rarely goes amiss and which so often is an integral part of a shared fishing experience. You take your turn and, when it comes, you fish as if your very life depended on it but not at the expense of the next man, whose turn is surely to come. Angling, especially on hard-fished club water is a shared experience. It is surely the stamp of a maturing angler that he gets as much pleasure from the success of his companion as he does from the catching of fish to his own rod. It is a great sense of comfort that, as age will surely deny us long hours with rod in hand, we shall get as much pleasure watching the fate of fellow anglers as we did previously from our own efforts.

And this is where the second, different but related issue comes to mind. My distillation of Bill Currie's writings was profound but not always accurate, none more so than my application of flies to fishing methods and circumstances. I was thrilled by the very names of flies such as Zulu and Coch-Y-Bondhu. These are enormously evocative names that have imbued the imagination of anglers for generations. They convey something of the mystique and heritage of the whole experience, way beyond the rational choice of their usage in diverse circumstances. And this is where I became seriously derailed. I had read of – and adopted – these undoubted killers and had attributed them with near infallible status. The thought that they might best be restricted to the peaty waters of the north had not entered my head. So, it was against this background of naive conviction that I painstakingly tied three-fly casts of Coch-Y-Bondhu and Zulu on to five-inch droppers of five-pound nylon, complemented by the addition of one very large Greenwell's Glory on the point. Now, at best, this combination might have been of marginal interest on a very windy day on some lochan in north-west Sutherland. It was hardly the most promising combination for the clear waters of Gala, which were my destination. So, it was with the utmost enthusiasm and the grossest of ignorance that I set forth for Stow with tackle that had taken me a brief lifetime to accumulate and all of which was completely inappropriate.

I had reached the age of young independence when bus rides to the Borders were sanctioned by persuasive assurance of careful wading and common sense. (How trusting parents can sometimes be!) The opportunities were few but when they did arise, I seized them with the conviction of the damned. I joined that band of swashbuckling pirates who roamed the streets of Edinburgh to Gala, whose trademark identity was the pavement gait of those for whom rolled-down thigh waders conferred an essential bandiness as if striving to stay upright on some pitching schooner in the Caribbean. Having done it once, it became a habit that no measure of scornful ridicule could dislodge. From Edinburgh to Gala, the gang assembled with the pirates from Eskbank and Gorebridge being progressively deposited at Heriot, Fountainhall and Stow. And I learnt a lot on these bus journeys. I heard the utter conviction associated with the use of a size eighteen dry Badger-and-Red countered by the infallibility of a fourteen Snipe-and-Purple in clearing water, not to mention the necessity of fishing small Greenwells, dry and wet. Magic – all of it – to young ears! So, when I stumbled off the bus at Stow, it was with the conviction of one who could not fail; one of the informed brotherhood who had come to pillage the clear waters of the south.

I was soon to learn that unbounded enthusiasm was no match for gross ignorance – and this was a hard lesson! Because, for all my conviction to the contrary, the trout of Gala Water showed a remarkable reluctance to rise to size ten Zulus and Coch-Y-Bondhus, not least on five-pound nylon! Now quite how all this might have ended, I am not sure but for the intervention of my ten-minute mentor. I can see him yet, a man in black, switching his flies across the stream beside Stow Inn. And he must have seen me and recognised a would-be angler in need of much help. He did not fuss, he was not critical and he was not condescending. He replaced my cast of Highland atrocities with a length of three-pound nylon to which he attached a short dropper. He attached two size-sixteen Greenwell's at short spacing and – crucially – said I would now catch fish! Not only that, he quietly enthused about the two-pounder he had taken on this very pool only the week before – the pool he was now vacating for myself. He could do nothing for the makeshift rod, reel and line that were mine and he had the presence of mind not even to hint at their inadequacy. Everything about this man was quietly positive and he treated me as an equal who just required a helping hand. And he was right – I did catch a fish – not a two-pounder but a perfect burn trout of six ounces. It was the most exquisite of trout and of the utmost importance to me and my future as a fisherman. I now knew it was possible to catch trout and I could join in the bus talk about the day's catch! I remember my mentor making the briefest of appearances later in the day, quietly enquiring of my success. I now know that he would, of course, have taken as much pleasure in my modest success as I did. As the years have gone by, I too have had the greatest of pleasure in this sharing of flies and of showing some fellow angler the best taking spot in a pool. There is nothing particularly meritorious in this. It is just a manifestation of the morality and generosity of spirit that imbues the writings of men like Bill Currie. And it is the very essence of what true fishing companionship is all about.

Gala with its educated trout was to prove an uncompromising instructor in the years ahead. Success here depended on watercraft, crucially an understanding of where trout lie and how they could be approached without disturbance. In all but spate conditions, the streams were shallow and often fast, separating enticing glides of promise, whose vegetated banks provided cover but with the inevitably associated challenges of approach. Its devotees soon learned to improvise all manner of casting that would allow fly presentation in the likely spot – albeit for fleeting seconds before the fly would be swept and dragged askew – normally to be followed by fleeting shadows of mass exodus as the residents sought cover. It was the sort of place where wading required the utmost of stealth and where the slightest of bow waves would render further fishing useless. Better to move on and try elsewhere. It was free fishing and amazingly good value at that. The downside was that it was fished hard and the trout could be incredibly choosy but once you got into the way of things, you could catch them.

It was here that I honed any skills I have in fishing the dry fly. From the outset, I tied my own dry flies, with occasional purchases to complement my rough and ready collection tied from odds and ends of fur and feathers, the smaller the better. Two-pound tippets were the order of the day and it was generally a waste of time to fish heavier. By now, I was fishing a quality rod of hollow glass fibre with reel and line to match, all thanks to the generosity of my father. Once father got properly involved in anything, he always went for the best equipment he could afford. Now, he never pursued fishing as an interest for himself but he must have discerned that, for his son, fishing was becoming more than a passing interest – something more than a phase which he would outgrow. Whatever, I recall the day when father and I went to purchase a rod from the local tackle shop. The staff were their usual dour self but polite as ever. They had no need to communicate that much because I knew what I wanted – a nine-foot, hollow glass rod of reasonable price – whose make I cannot recall. I am sure it would have served me admirably but father sought advice and – credit to the staff – they were not slow in giving it! I left that shop, the proud owner of a Hardy Jet with matching Marquis reel. At that time, you could not do much better! Now, price is certainly not everything in fishing tackle. None of my subsequent rods has, in a relative sense, been in a similar price bracket but the

Hardy Jet was some performer. I fished it for years until its sad demise in the boot hinges of my car. It was like losing a friend and, when I could afford it, I bought its replacement with which, on occasion, I still fish. It seems a bit soft in action by today's standards in rod fashion but it can still do the business. With a little more care than I gave its predecessor, it should outlive its owner.

With the appropriate tackle, and an increasing awareness of watercraft, I could now do serious damage to trout stocks on the Gala! In truth, the opportunities were somewhat restricted but of the occasions I could manage, the memories are fond. These were formative years, exploring dressings, where dark olives and their smaller lighter brethren later in the season prompted innovation. This was also the time when I read avidly in J. L. Harris's *An Angler's Entymology* – what a useful book! Dressings were given and inspiration issued to explore variation in form and colour, where season and diurnal variation in light and temperature dictated. Small shifts in size and pattern could render a dressing such as Greenwell's Glory quite ubiquitous. I was fascinated by thoughts on how changes in the surface density (numbers) of flies of different species might result in a switch in feeding behaviour of trout from one species to another. I once tested this to the extreme by throwing grass seed in the wind from the suspension bridge across the Tweed at Melrose. I have never seen a more spectacular rise of trout! It was as if every fish downstream of the bridge gave up on what it had previously been targeting and focussed on the new manna from heaven – try it sometime! I learnt to catch fish on dry Olives – patterns akin to Hare's Ear and the like, as well as Badgers and Grey Hens. There are fishers who would not be seen dead without a Grey Hen and Rusty but, strangely, it was never top of my list. It did damage on the Tweed and seemed to be particularly effective on some smaller rivers in the east. Whatever, the overriding message seemed to be: Fish small and fine, try variations in shading of dressings and, crucially, approach with care!

Years later, I was to return one evening to the Gala with my two sons, neither of whom had fished for river trout. The evening was perfect – a fining water in fading sunlight in early July. I do not recall how many fish were caught but I could not fail (Blue-Upright dressings, as I recall). I have very fond memories of my younger son and I taking a string of trout – nothing particularly large but all were of fantastic quality – from a shaded run before darkness settled. Nothing had changed on the Gala in the intervening twenty years. If you were fortunate to get it right and had a modicum of skill, the trout were there to be caught. I assume it is still the case that it yields its trout to those who persevere. Another thirty years have passed and I have never returned – and probably never shall – the memories are too precious to be sullied by clumsy failure. There again, I now have grandchildren and they too might want to fish. What better place to start than this delightful border stream?

I suppose I stopped fishing the Gala when enticed by its larger brother – the Tweed. The expectation – and the reality – was that the fish would be bigger. This almost seems insulting to the Gala but I hope to have said enough in its praises to indicate otherwise. The Gala is a fine stream but the Tweed – although related – is a very different fishing experience. It has streams within streams and glides within glides. Everything is scaled up and part of the secret to success in its fishing is to dissemble its large volume into manageable streams and lies. It demands watercraft but, strangely, not to the same extent as the smaller Gala. No doubt, fish are still scared off by clumsy wading but the angler can still succeed by throwing a longer line to fish at distance in a manner not possible on a smaller stream. There may be more subtle differences in acceptable approach that relate to depth and fields of vision. I regularly caught Tweed trout on a dry fly floated downstream from my rod tip close to where I stood – a practice which was rarely successful on the shallower Gala.

I fished the Tweed mostly at Melrose on the St Helen's stretch of the local angling club and, over the years, did best on the stretch at the neck of the stream running into the flats above the old weir. I did fish in the summer but most of my effort was in the springtime, particularly in the months of April and May. Late June and July brought on the evening fishing and – reputedly – it could be outstanding. However, I left this largely unexplored because, by this time, my summer attention was being turned increasingly to the hill lochs of Sutherland. So, for me, Tweed trout were spring trout – and what good fish they could be! I have spent freezing days in snow flurries and sleet showers punctuated by glorious minutes of warm sunshine. Occasionally, these sunny interludes would last long enough for my numbed hands to thaw sufficiently that I could strip line and wind it in as required. Often it was more a comedy of errors as I would try desperately to keep contact with a plunging fish in the fast flow. These interludes were the occasion of sporadic and phenomenal hatches of March Brown. It was quite extraordinary how such shifts in weather would trigger a change in hatching behaviour and the feeding behaviour of trout, just as Harris had intimated. They would slash with relish at the armada of mottled-brown sails rushing downstream in bursts of sunlight. If I was lucky, I might have two in the bag before the next wintry shower defied the arrival of summer. If my luck was in, the whole sequence would be repeated many times from mid-morning to early afternoon. It was always a time to be selective in what was kept but some of the trout were in remarkably good condition, presumably benefiting partly from the feast of Dark Olives and March Browns.

If the weather was not too inclement, I would sit under one of the large willows and await the next burst of activity. No doubt, I was wasting a fishing opportunity in not getting to grips with nymph fishing at various depths, as so masterfully practiced by grayling fishers. However, for me, trout fishing is all about catching fish up top. I may not catch as many fish as might otherwise be the case but the approach seems to match my enjoyment of the pursuit. I recall one occasion when, sitting, eating and drinking and trying to keep warm, I spotted a good fish rise close to my bank some thirty metres upstream. There had been few rises that morning, so the opportunity of encountering a surface-feeding fish was not to be ignored. March Browns had not been hatching and I was fishing a dressing of the Large Dark Olive. I was rapidly in position some ten metres below the fish and, having noted the spot carefully started to lengthen line. It was one of those occasions where, partly because the fish had risen in quieter water behind a breakwater close to my bank, I expected to get one – and probably only one – shot at the fish. If the cast was good and the fly floated over the lie without undue drag, I knew there was a good chance of the trout taking this dressing. As luck would have it, the cast was up to the job and the most almighty swirl was followed by a wicked plunging of the rod tip as I bent into the largest river trout I had hooked. It had no intention of hanging around the breakwater and was soon stationed, boring deeply in midstream some twenty metres upstream from where I stood in excitement, bracing myself against its repeated writhing. Now, I had by this juncture hooked and landed many trout from Gala and Tweed but I had still to break the pound mark – a sort of holy grail in the development of a trout fisher. There was no doubt that the opportunity to do so was now mine. I credit myself with doing everything appropriately during the following minutes. I kept the fish moving but was not excessively hard on it. I kept the line tight but was in no danger of being smashed – at least, I hoped not – and, after the initial surge of panic, I had got control of the situation. It was only a matter of time and I would make the fish my own. A few minutes more and the fish showed and started to wallow in the quieter water, close to the lie from which it was hooked. It was massive and stunningly magnificent. It was now only a matter of easing it over the net and lifting it cleanly to the bank. But the net was not there. It lay, of course beside my bag under the willow, some twenty metres away. This was to be my first experience of walking a fish to where I wished it. I have done this subsequently many times with salmon and it is nearly always an easy thing to do – the fish will quietly follow where you lead. And this trout was no exception. It followed obediently as I edged my way downstream. Then, net in hand, I gently but purposefully drew the fish towards the mesh. And, it was at this point, that the hook-hold gave and the largest river trout I had ever hooked, swam slowly to the depths. The veil was restored, the fish had won its freedom and I was left disconsolate. I have never subsequently hooked a bigger river trout and probably never shall. I have hooked and landed large trout when fishing for salmon and the experience has always been disappointing. The tackle has been a mismatch for the size of fish – and many of them have been several pounds in weight – but not as big as my Tweed trout on the Dark Olive. Hooking such fish on salmon gear is unsatisfactory. It is as if a mistake has been made. But hooking such monsters by design on trout tackle is quite another matter.

I fished Tweed for trout on other occasions but not often after the loss of the big trout. This had nothing to do with my enthusiasm for the challenge but, quite inadvertently, my fishing attention was being led elsewhere. It was all a matter of opportunity and, progressively, since my early successes on Gala and Tweed, my summers were becoming increasingly focussed on the capture of loch trout. The attraction of Sutherland hill lochs was gradually outweighing that of river fishing and – deep down – I now know what I have sensed for a long time, namely that river fishing for trout is something that I cherish but also something to which I may well never return. However, the memories are good and with these, I shall continue to dream.

Sutherland Discovered

My introduction to Sutherland was the seemingly endless car journey from Lairg in the east to the far north-west Highlands. In those days, it took a full twelve hours to travel by car from Edinburgh to the scattered crofts of this remote part. Having arrived in Lairg, it was not entirely unreasonable to assume that the journey was nearly over; the postal address was, after all, 'by Lairg'. However, in terms of journey time and distance, this was a bit of a misnomer. There remained a full fifty miles of tortuous single-track road that could take up to three hours of travel time. The whole highway has, of course, changed over the years and journey times have been greatly reduced. The main A9 route from Edinburgh to Inverness has long boasted stretches of motorway to Perth and the very mixed blessing of mostly dual carriageway and sporadic two-way stretches of trunk road north of Perth. The number of crashes and indeed fatalities on this blend of road systems has led to an ongoing call for the whole stretch to be 'dualled'. Today, the mostly single-track stretch to the north-west of Lairg has been vastly improved – a somewhat anomalous occurrence given the persistent decline in the population of its far-flung communities over the past century.

Heading north-west from Lairg was a completely new venture for my family. We travelled the long and foreboding length of Loch Shin with its rolling waves. Breakers crashed on to its shingle shores with exposed tree stumps that shone ash-silver in the hard afternoon light. Shin is a hydro water and, at low summer levels, its desolate shores hint at what must have been a very different and more pleasing landscape of steep-sided valley and river. It has long been flooded but the whole scene is still one of raw destruction. Its pounding waves and shifting water levels have meant that, even now, Shin has only sparse vegetation on its shores. It is all very bleak. Keep traveling north past the waters at Merkland and you eventually reach the watershed between east and west. Here the weather can change markedly, being often cloudy and wet to the west and drier and sunnier to the east. It can, of course, be the opposite and, on the very first occasion that

I crossed this pass from east to west, the skies cleared. The sun shone brightly on the magic waters of Stack and More with the beguiling River Laxford threading its way to its sheltered estuary on the Atlantic coast. These were waters of high repute, waters that were the preserve of the privileged few. They were amongst the very best of sea trout and salmon fisheries and were patently inaccessible to most fishers. At the time, it required not only money but connection if you were to fish these waters. Off-road parking at the top end of Loch Stack was the preserve of Rolls and Bentley and it was a rare and almost embarrassing sight to find a lesser make of car parked near these waters!

Things have changed considerably. The west coast sea-trout runs have been vastly diminished to the point of near extinction and the salmon stock is now much depleted. This demise is common to most of the west-coast fisheries and represents a sad and shameful misuse of a resource. As a nation, we have allowed governmental support of salmon farming in western coastal waters that has almost certainly been massively detrimental to the natural migratory stock and its welfare. This could be reversed but it would require a change in governmental policy, basically an admission that the promotion of salmon farming as currently practised has not been entirely wise and needs amending. As these once-exclusive fisheries have declined, their accessibility to the public has increased. Days – indeed weeks – can now be arranged though hotels and estates. Gone is the predominance of Rolls and Bentley by the waterside. But, of course, anglers will not match the phenomenal catches of years gone by. In fact, any sea trout that might now be caught will be returned to the water; the same holds true of most salmon. What a tragedy that things should have come to this. It truly is something of a disgrace that more robust intervention has not been forthcoming. The reasons for decline in stock may be somewhat complex but, where some causes are apparent and no action is taken, then we have a shared responsibility for environmental damage. In the end, we vote for the decision makers and we have a responsibility to question and inform their policy. Our silence on these matters makes us complicit to the inadequacy of current policy. I may not mourn the passing of the once exclusive nature of these fisheries. Exclusive they indeed were, although a polite enquiry regarding preserved fishing could often result in a positive and welcome invitation to fish by arrangement. I do not know if that was ever the case on the Laxford waters but it most certainly was elsewhere. What I do mourn, however, is the passing of the resource as such.

Stack and More are wild waters but not quite as foreboding and bleak as Shin. They do not have the same length of water for the massive build-up of spray-whipped rollers. But the strong north-westerlies do funnel down the length of these formidable waters and the waves are often fearsome. It was the relatively shallow and sheltered bays at either end of the lochs that were the favoured fishing spots. It was here that boats were carefully managed and drifts held by ghillies who knew the water. I may never have fished these waters but I have spent hours, from the shelter of some nook or cranny on the surrounding slopes of Fionavon, Arkle or Stack, watching the drifts of boats and their fishers. From these glorious vantage points, I have spied on the efforts of ghillies and rods alike and watched in thrilled envy as bent rods led fish to the waiting net. What a sight! I often wondered if I did not get as much pleasure from just watching these wild tussles, as did the rods who paid so dearly to participate. It was all very exciting but seemingly inaccessible.

The final few miles to the north-west from Laxford Bridge are at once amongst the most stunning and yet disarming you can travel in mainland Britain. There are no trees, not because you are above the tree line but because of the extensive open grazing by sheep and deer and the prevailing Atlantic blast. These agents combine to prevent any semblance of regeneration other than the development of meagre patches of low scrub. The landscape is predominantly one of rock and water interspersed with moorland grasses and low shrubs. Ancient gneiss boulders and outcrops shine pink in the evening light of a summer's day, contrasting starkly with the dark peat-stained waters, everything from glorified puddles to full-blown lochs. In season, their bays come alive with the massive flowers of white and yellow water-lily. At other times, bog cotton and pondweeds add more splashes of vibrant colour to the glistening scene. Every twist and turn on the road reveals a new and shining perspective as the sun sets lower in the western sky. Further to the west, the vast panorama of Inchard and the far Atlantic beckons. A glance to the rear shows Fionavon and Arkle glowing pink with wispy white clouds topping their ridges. The evening starts to cool and the blueness of the sky fades. Everything to the west is blinding and dazzling in the setting sun and everything behind and to the east is in pastel shades and satin finish. What a glorious sight!

And, just as you are coming to terms with the unusual and unexpected majesty of the place, the final mile beckons down towards the rocky promontories and dunes of a stunning Atlantic storm beach. For millennia, the silver sands have raced hard in the prevailing on-shore storm and sculpted a massive dune front, fixed for a time by encroaching marram grass. But here, it is all change. The next storm will shred or bury the marram and shift the front and the sculpture will be different; always the same theme of drifting, tapering shoulders of sand but always subtly new in its expression. As if to confirm your very arrival in the place, you can stand at the wave front with your feet wet in the Atlantic surf and marvel at the pink and blue pastel reflections of the evening sky on a thin and watery lacework of foam and dark wet sand. As the next wave races to cover your feet, all to the deafening cacophony of crashing rollers, you can lift your eyes to the distant horizon and above. If you stay long enough and darkness encroaches, you will be startled by the first of the night's shooting stars. Even today, as I did fifty years ago, it is most likely that you will stand transfixed at the unutterable beauty of the place as the evening chill encroaches. It is also most likely that you will do so in the contentment of complete and utter solitude. Such is north-west Sutherland.

Those early years in Sutherland were ones of exceptional weather. Scotland is hardly a place renowned for its sunshine and warmth and yet, on occasion, it can provide just that – day after day of consistently clear skies; days of sun and scorching heat. Such was the weather of my first two summers in the far north-west. For days, the temperatures soared and, of course, the waters shrank. Because such weather is unusual, the west coast is hardly over-populated with tourists. So, when the sun shines for days on end and a heat wave occurs, the few tourists who are travelling in the region find themselves in an area of outstanding beauty with essentially sole access to its glorious sandy beaches. It does get hot! By early afternoon, any welcome morning cool is dispelled as the sun climbs high in a relentlessly blue sky. Asphalt is running on tarred roads and, as you approach the beaches, the dry dunes burn your feet – quite literally. Here, the coastal Atlantic water is never warm but, in the prevailing and prolonged calm, there are always extensive pockets of warmer water that have not mixed with the cooler mass. Find these pockets and you have found your own private, heated swimming pool for days on end – always shifting, of course, with the tidal water. What a place!

Now, in these first years, none of this exceptional heat was, of course, conducive to good trout fishing. But, because these were my first visits to the place, I had no real appreciation, beyond that gleaned from what I had read, of what I was missing. At the time and to this day, I would not have traded these first two years of summer heat and drought for anything in the fishing world; they were just glorious and happy times. In later years, having tasted the joys of better trout fishing in these parts, I would have been increasingly frustrated by the incessant sunshine and warmth of those early visits. At the time, I confined any efforts at catching trout to sorties on the local burn. The trout were small and dark but I was content with what they offered. I knew roughly what I was about and soon could guarantee a supply of breakfast fish. They were not great eating but, as ever, my family obliged! I could have done much better, of course, had I been more adaptable. I had this fixation, from what I had read of Sutherland, of fishing with large flies, so a selection of unnecessarily large Silver and Kingfisher Butchers were cast at the unsuspecting inhabitants of the burn. I doubt if they had previously seen an artificial fly and I doubt if they will have seen one since.

During my first visit, I caught flounders on a spoon and worm, casting into the low-tide water of the sandy beach. At high tide, I caught mackerel, pollack and coalfish on the spinner from the rocky promontories of the bay. One evening, I watched transfixed as a shoal of pollack was split in two by a fast-pursuing seal in the deep green waters at my feet. And one night, after stormy weather, a large whale surfaced in the bay. I should have fished more in the sea when conditions were pretty much ideal but I have no regrets. I enjoyed what I did and was slowly building an assurance in my fishing and a love for this place that came to fruition in later years.

My early joy in Sutherland was found in much more than its stark beauty. It was firmly bedded in its people and in none more so than Alec and his wife Maggie-Anne. These dear people were already in their later years when we first met. They were crofting folk and had been brought up in this far-flung community. Their kindness and interest in me as a person seemed to have no bounds. Despite my young years, Alec sought my opinion – and I sought his – on topical matters, mostly political and not least those pertaining to Scotland as a nation state. Many was the hour that he would lean on his scythe as we cut and dried hay together; cutting the sweet meadow grass in the morning sun, turning it and drying it on nets stretched over stone dykes before stacking. I can see his lean and scrawny body clearly, his craggy jaw chewing on tobacco, as he would contemplate some pressing point of news. An eventual pronouncement would be punctuated by a routine spit before his face would lighten and the warm dignity of his smile would prevail. He was an intelligent man whose education was based largely on his life experience. He had travelled during the Great War and had disarming stories of far-off places. He was tough; his picture as a boxer in the Navy adorned his mantelpiece but his hardness was strictly confined to a determination and life style that ensured survival in this declining community. To me, he never showed anything but a welcoming countenance. Maggie-Anne had been in service as a young girl at Munlochy House in the Black Isle, a few miles from where I grew up as a child. They were the most generous of people and I adored them for the affection they showed me and my family. I cherish their memory.

On my second visit, I had most definitely planned loch fishing. Alec had enthused me with tales of how the retired, seemingly reclusive general who could be ranked as one of his nearest neighbours would, out of preference, fish the local loch for salmon rather than its illustrious neighbours in the Laxford catchment. I suppose that I must have made the naive assumption that, if the local loch was good for salmon, then it must surely be good for trout. Not only had I planned my assault in terms of fishing tackle – rod and line and flies to match – but I had embarked on my one and only attempt to seriously study what trout were eating. I assume that this was with a view to being better informed in the ways of trout and, therefore, being better equipped for their capture. So, as well as transporting the usual fishing paraphernalia, I ventured north with formalin solution and storage vials for the stomach contents of trout – all very laudable for a budding biologist! Now, this whole escapade coincided with my childish determination to pursue a hands-on approach to the study of life. It was a time when I had leaf-litter frames scattered around my father's garden so that I could monitor litter consumption by earthworms as a function of soil temperature. It was the year when I requested a dissection kit and a dogfish for Christmas – perhaps not the most popular request of the festive season. One end of the kitchen table was reserved for serving turkey, the other end was a cross between gutting station and fish morgue! The choice on the menu was turkey with trimmings or – if you had the stomach for it – dog fish and formalin. The whole kitchen stank of dogfish and formaldehyde; health and safety was apparently not in vogue! Things freshened up a bit in spring when I tried, with mixed success, to hatch trout eggs to the alevin stage. This was not a great success and, in retrospect, I suspect we had a major problem with zinc or lead in our water supply. At any rate, the idea of accumulating stomach contents of trout and having a look-see at what they were eating seemed perfectly normal and acceptable. The whole venture was a bit disappointing because I found it inordinately difficult to make sense of the diverse insect body parts. In the end, I only examined a smallish number of all the collected samples. I hate to reflect on the disposal of the remaining specimen tubes.

On these first visits to Sutherland, the local loch did not yield large trout but numbers of smaller fish were there to be caught and I continued to learn and improve as a caster of flies and catcher of fish – nothing spectacular but enough to keep me going. I fished the standard selection of loch flies, all bought and mostly too gaudy and over-dressed. I probably fished too large, except on the bob where something bushier would have been appropriate. This most critical of positions on the cast was graced by a Coch-Y-Bondhu. Something of that ilk was, after all, recommended for these peaty waters. However, it was only later that I appreciated how poorly dressed was the shop dressing that I fished. It was a near two-dimensional, scrawny misrepresentation of the real thing that I would soon be tying in the ensuing winter months. My own dressing would have all the kick and subtle vibrancy that the shop tying lacked. However, I did catch fish and soon found some favoured points and bays. It was all bank fishing and, as I tramped around the rocky shores, I found storm-debris of what once must have been the old general's boat. These sad remains spoke of a better time that, at least for the general, was now past – a time when no doubt many a high drama was enacted along the drop-off from the sand bar at the far end of the loch. I know now that this would have been choice territory for salmon and, during these early years, stale residents from the early summer run would occasionally splash noisily in this bay – all very exciting but quite uncatchable then as now.

It was the following year before I ventured further inland and fished the loch that fed the general's favourite water. The weather in this and subsequent years was less extreme in terms of sun, heat and drought and the surrounding moors came alive with fresh and intense colours as I tramped their course. The connecting burn between this and the general's loch was tiny but most certainly would have allowed the passage of salmon along its tortuous length. I tried different parts of this more inland water but, in the end, concentrated most of my efforts on its top bay. This was more of an inlet than a full-blown bay and it did seem to hold large numbers of free-rising fish. Years later, I found a better size of fish in other parts of the loch but, initially, it was the relative abundance of smaller fish that attracted me to it.

On hot summer days and invigorated by the surge of cold Atlantic breakers, I would depart the scorching sands of the coast and head for the hills with keen anticipation and an eager step. I tramped these parts wearing the same worn jeans, shirt and jersey for years, fresh and invigorated from the sea and feeling at ease in clothes that had been steeped in sphagnum bogs and heather and, in later years, washed frequently in torrents of rain. There did not seem much point in wearing a jacket because, at that time, I could not afford one that would both breathe and keep me dry. Better to get soaked by rain blowing in from the Atlantic and then let the ever-present wind and any sunshine bonus effect a quick drying. My boots were worn but comfortable having tramped many miles. Their laces were fashioned from twine ditched by trawlers and washed up on the local storm beach. Occasionally – when I remembered – I might stuff a trusty and increasingly decrepit nylon cape into my bag. This was mostly useless for keeping me dry but it provided a further bit of shelter when the wind truly blew. It also had the intriguing property of acting like a sail and, with a following wind, the homeward journey could be covered at a fair rate of knots!

I always travelled light; no encumbrances of excess tackle for me! My rod, a small bag with odds and ends of tackle and a net sufficed. I used to tramp the hills with a long-handled net that had seen service on the banks of the Tweed and had a lowland pebble from that catchment stuck in its hollow base. Some forty years later, I lost this friend of a net – we belonged to one another following many close adventures with fish – when it was knocked overboard in a favourite loch. It will still be in the depths of that water but our time together has, regrettably, long passed. It was a very cheap and basic net but, crucially, it doubled as a staff when I strove to make rapid progress over rough moorland. Rapid, nimble footwork, hopping on drier stones and mossy hummocks, whilst leaping over slippery bogs and hollows, was the order of the day. These were the days when I learnt to distinguish between sphagnum species that indicated drier hummocks and those – especially the lush green ones – that indicated treacherous bog. It was all about moving rapidly and safely over awkward ground where sprained ankles or worse were a real possibility.

On that first occasion, in great anticipation, I put up my rod. A Coch-Y-Bondhu graced the bob and, although I cannot swear to it, a Black Pennel was most likely on the tail. Over the years, nearly all my fish were taken on the bob, making the tail pattern pretty much redundant. The tail pattern generally served as a means of anchoring the bob, helping to keep it in and about the surface. The bob would skid and jump but generally not for long because it was such an attractor of fish that often it would be attacked with gusto as soon as it hit the water. This was exciting fishing! It sufficed to lay a fine line on the water, often diagonally across the wind. The line would start to bow in the wind as the rod tip was lifted and the bob would start to skid. Then came the swirl and another fish would be hooked! The Coch-Y-Bondhu was incredibly effective. It did best in a good steady wind – no wave was too big – if I could keep the fly in the water. Sunshine or broken cloud was always better than dull weather and daytime was always better than the later evening when the sun was down. How good was it really? Well, I have taken not just hundreds but thousands of trout on this pattern during fifty years of fishing. This is not meant to be boastful. Indeed, many anglers will have taken a lot more trout than I. Because I have fished this fly to the exclusion of many others, it has inevitably caught most of my fish. I was in the habit of dressing this fly as large as possible; hackle fibres of at least one inch in length were not too long. The contrasting pale and dark colouring of the red-black furnace hackle seemed to be a winner and, combined with its bulky thorax of peacock herl, a generous gold tinsel tag and red-silk head – all on a size ten forged hook – the fly was a killer.

For me, the little loch and its promontory became a proving ground; a water where, with no critical eyes upon me, I became a loch fisher. Some of my casting was erratic and atrocious (you must start somewhere) but I did catch fish. I also hooked a great deal of heather and spent a vast amount of time frustrated in the unravelling of wind knots and the inevitable tying of new casts. For brief and glorious spells though, I was master of the situation and, against the majestic panoramic background of sky and hills, I could make the bob fly dance in the wind and waves. Wonder of wonders, trout would rise to these creations of hackle and tinsel; rise to these great warrior flies whose romantic heritage was distilled from the wild peaty waters of north-west Sutherland. The rises were fast, aggressive grabs at things I had created – flies that were my expression of a glorious tradition. Fish after fish – an apparently endless supply – revealed their small gold and red flanks in the sunlit waves, like flags of declaration that what I was doing was not all wrong. Bit by bit, in fishing the bob fly, I was no longer a novice. I still may have had much to learn but I had been well and truly initiated into the ranks of loch fishermen.

So, in many ways, my apprenticeship as angler was complete. I could never again be so painstakingly slow to adapt my ways to a new fishing challenge.

Hooks and casts, weights and floats, lines and reels and rods were now familiar things. Their permutations of use were endless and any awareness of this could surely represent progress. But my introduction to Sutherland was much more than this because it was a time that coincided with the awakening of intellect and emotions to the things that were ultimately of importance to me as a person. It was a flourishing of things sown in my early childhood. It was a time when I grew up and developed an independent and critical mind, an awareness based more on knowledge and less on ignorance. It was a time for increased conviction, freedom of expression and compassion. It was a time when I grew to love solitude and the natural beauty of things. All these things were a growing part of what became 'me' and all of this happened on the moors and waters of Sutherland, because I wanted to be a fisher. When all is said and done, I can find no more important reason to promote fishing in such wild places, than that it may help a person find meaning, contentment and joy in what, otherwise, is the pretty confusing and disturbing experience of 'life'. It surprises me not one bit that many people, who have otherwise demanding and stressful commitments, should also be ardent fishers. No surprise there at all.

Sutherland Revisited

One day, I kept walking high on the rough grassy ridge above the little loch with its small bay. I had mixed feelings about giving this small water a miss, trudging with my sights set on distant ridges where new frontiers now beckoned. Alec seemed surprised that I had not ventured further and that I was apparently content to catch small fish. Perhaps because of his reminiscing – perhaps through a sense of my not having heeded his advice – I now headed for the higher lochs of which he spoke. However, it was with a sense of unease, perhaps one of regret and sneaking disloyalty, that I passed the small bay with its stony promontory. I gave it a scant but fond glance from a grassy ridge. I knew it to be a near certainty that, in the prevailing wind and sunshine, I could have caught fish from the promontory – a lot of them – but now the higher lochans beckoned with their reputation for bigger fish. This was a reputation based on the experience of previous generations. But why should the fishing have changed much in these remote parts from sixty years previously? After all, the hills and the water surely had not changed greatly in the intervening years. I say this with some confidence because the extreme north-west appears to have escaped the devastation associated with acid rain in more southerly quarters.

The climb was steep and the ground rough. Massive and ancient boulders of pink and grey gneiss shone with a hard defiance; great lumps of erratic debris from a receding glacier twelve thousand years ago. A pause for breath on the steep ascent gave opportunity to look back and down on vast hazy views of tumbling moors and lochs towards the sheer bulk of islands in a glistening sea. Further up the hill and looking down to the north-west, a stunning view of bright golden sand stranded the distant white breakers of the blue-green ocean. This is a place where, if you climb to the hilltops, the conglomerate is sculpted and scarred massively in the line of glacial retreat. Long tables and parallel benches of reddish pebble stone are aligned as if in preparation for some great outdoor banquet. It is a truly extraordinary sight: the remnant of a vast land mass, once formed from deep sediments deposited on top of the ancient gneiss bed and then, in more recent times, shredded under the massive weight of moving ice.

It is a place that, over the years never failed to surprise. On two occasions, I stumbled across a family of badgers that bolted to the safety of a great pile of gneiss rocks on a downward slope. Presumably, that is where they had their sett. Their life experience must have been very different from that of badgers in the more sedate fringes of farm and woodland hundreds of miles to the south. What on earth did they eat? Presumably, plant matter was the main diet, maybe supplemented by the occasional frog or bird egg. There did not seem to be much else to hand. Can badgers catch and eat trout?

Every dip in this landscape, every rocky hollow with its encroaching black peat, is water-filled. The whole vista is one of glistening puddles and lochans of all sizes, interlaced by a web of sparse vegetation, rocky outcrops and boulders. Some of these lochans are tiny – a few tens of yards across – others are more substantial. Most hold trout and most of these are impoverished dark fingerlings. The surprise is that trout should be there at all, forming part of the life that has persisted in such tiny acid pools. Some waters appear to contain no fish whatsoever and some continue to surprise with very few fish but of much bigger size. The occasional almighty pull at a wayward fly from some passing uncommitted cast is always a rude awakening!

This is a place where my boots would land on ground that may never previously have been tramped. For years, there would have been annual sorties from shepherds rounding up sheep from the common grazing, always in advance of the long tramp to the lamb sales in the east. But the number of trekkers would be so few that most of the ground was effectively virgin territory for tramping. Alec's brother would have been one of those who brought in the sheep from the hill and no doubt my feet followed closely those of his and others from past generations, especially around loch shores. However, the ground is so rugged without any hint of beaten tracks beyond the habitual wanderings of sheep that the overall experience is one of exploration. In all the times I wandered there, I never met another soul, beyond the occasional companion whom I had invited to share this special place. I knew, through here-say over the years, that others had frequented these parts but I never met them on the moor or at the lochs. I am sure it would have detracted from the experience for us both, had I stumbled on another lone angler in the wild. It was a place where you would cast to trout that had never seen a fly before, trout that had no previous experience of lines, nylon and hooks. These were the sorts of waters where, so long as you did not clatter around on the shore and, so long as you did not splash the line on the forward cast, it was a near certainty that you would catch fish.

On my first ascent, I came quite suddenly upon the small lochans, peering down at the middle water nestled beneath a foreboding cliff face. The loch was a long thin stretch of peaty blackness, rippled from west to east. A small, round lochan could be glimpsed glistening to the west, separated from the middle water by a short heather-covered tumble of scree. I knew that, tucked away to the east and at a slightly higher elevation was the smallest of the three waters. To be seen, this loch required a further climb. At first glance, this third lochan was quite unassuming but, as with many things, first appearance was to prove deceptive. From the far shores of the three waters rose a sharp cliff of conglomerate that danced red-brown in the sunlight. It rose from the water some hundred feet or more in height. Over the years its weathered face had released an avalanche of scree that was now well covered by low moorland vegetation. Only the occasional erratic boulder of conglomerate, shining and starkly free of plant cover, indicated that the formation of this landscape was still a work in progress. This stunning visual imagery was complemented by sounds of a strangely melancholy nature, the musical score that is often associated with such wild places. I would hear the wind racing through grass and heather and the incessant lapping of waves on rocky and peaty shores. These persistent voices were punctuated by the lonely sporadic tweeting of late nesting wheatears and larks as they flitted ahead of my approaching footfall. The aggressive and startled croaking of ravens declared ownership of the cliff face and, occasionally, a percussive rumbling announced a further addition of scree. In the distance, could be heard the forlorn bleating of sheep. But nearly always, the symphony was dominated by the singing wind in the grass and heather; always the wind.

On my first visit, I found the fish to be bigger – but not substantially so – than in the lower lochs which had been my nursery. Fish of six to eight ounces were the norm but they fought exceedingly hard and would readily speed line from the reel whilst bowing the rod and line hard against the wind – all very exciting! I did catch bigger fish but only occasionally – twelve ounces was probably my best in those early forays. I soon found my favourite spots and learnt that some shores were more productive than others. One bay seemed devoid of fish but perhaps it was home to a few monsters. My favourite shoreline was the western stretch under the cliff. If you happen to tramp these shores, you will have

63

come to the right spot when your foot lands on the one wobbly flag of pebble stone. Fish abound in this western bay and object strongly to being deceived by the likes of you and me. I have fished this loch on numerous occasions over a great many years and found that the taking spots have remained pretty much the same. However, the size of fish has varied over the years – some years yielding beautifully marked fish up to fourteen ounces; other years have produced darker and smaller fish. I did find that, in the earlier season (late May to June; you do not want to be here too early), a more deeply sunk tail fly would take over from the bob fly as being most effective. Teal and Red, with a reddish-brown gamecock hackle, was particularly effective in these cooler waters. Otherwise, the Coch-Y-Bondhu never failed, given sufficient light, warmth and wind. Fortunately, these conditions would normally prevail, at least for short spells during any visit. Indeed, it was often best to rest the water when the sun disappeared and cool scuds of wind sent shadows across the water surface. As soon as things settled down again, the trout would immediately respond, so no time was wasted when conditions were right. No doubt, if I had varied my tactics, I might have caught fish in less favourable conditions but my joy is in catching top feeders and I prefer to wait until conditions and fish oblige than pursue trout at all depths and costs; each to their own preference.

The small round loch to the west held smaller, darker fish and soon became less of a focus on my trips. The quality of sport on the middle loch far exceeded that of its western neighbour. During my early years, I rarely fished the smallest upper loch. This was because I found it to be completely devoid of fish. I never saw anything move on its surface and my half-hearted efforts proved fruitless. In retrospect, I find that my assessment of this smallest of waters was quite misplaced. My lack of early success was almost certainly attributable to the timing of my efforts. When things got tough on the middle loch – in other words, when conditions were not conducive to catching top feeders – I would tramp the extra yards and have a cast on the top loch. My early impressions were not favourable. It seemed to be a cold and uninviting prospect and so it was, given that the sun had disappeared behind racing grey clouds and the wind was funnelling down the water's length! It was hardly a fair trial of a lochan of which I had heard intriguing rumours. Quite inadvertently, I met someone (on the banks of the Tay, of all places) who had fished these waters and claimed to have caught a trout of some two-pound weight from the smallest of the lochs. For years, I was convinced that my source was mistaken. I assumed that his prize fish must have come from the productive middle water and that it was only a matter of time before I too would connect with one of these wild giants. The fact that my informant had been quite insistent that the water in question was the top loch had little bearing on my foolish judgement!

One day, for whatever reason, I decided to forego the pleasures of the middle water and fish the top water when conditions were good. It seemed a very different prospect as it glistened in the soft light of late afternoon with a mild westerly breeze rippling its surface. Its shores and narrow width dictated that stealth would be the order of the day. So, I took my time and cast carefully along its rugged banks. For some reason, I had foregone my usual floating-line tactics and bob-fly fixation (and about time too, I hear you say) and was fishing a slowly sinking line with a small (size fourteen) Grouse and Claret on the tail. When the fish took, it was with one almighty pull as line sped through my fingers and tore off the reel! A great golden flank caught the sunlight in the dark stained water and shot towards the safety of the far bank. It was a glorious moment of revelation and triumph when my net eventually engulfed this most beautiful of creatures. It was every bit the equal of my informant's account. What a glorious prize! The black and red markings on its sheen of golden flank were quite remarkable and so unexpected on a creature that, had it not been deceived by feathers and tinsel, would never have been revealed.

Over the years, I have caught many fish in these waters. The middle loch remains the most productive and the top loch produces the big ones and some of them are very big! It rarely yields many fish but they are always large and superbly marked. One of my acquaintances once returned a beautiful fish of some four-pounds weight, a superb trophy from such a small water. Subsequently, most of my fish from the top loch have succumbed to a bushy bob fly and many of the takes have been spectacular, although some have been deceptively gentle. But this wee loch does not always give of its best even when conditions look perfect. In fact, I am not sure that it always has a stock of fish. If it has, then I believe that sometimes the number of fish must be very small. I think that sometimes a few fish must be transported from the middle loch to the upper loch. I know of one acquaintance that, in his wisdom, did this very thing. But there may also be stocking through more natural agencies; I have sighted herons in the neighbourhood. There is also a distinct seepage of water from the top loch to the middle loch and I have a suspicion that this may on occasion become more of an underground burn and allow migration of sorts during the wet autumn and winter months. Whatever, I believe the stock is erratic and it may always have been so. Perhaps this was the water to which Alec referred when speaking of his brother's enthusiasm for the place but, at the time, I did not think to ask and, with the passing of time, the matter can only be one of fond speculation.

In the early years of my times in Sutherland, most of my fishing was from the banks of these small lochs. I had no incentive to explore further. As far as I was concerned, in finding this desolate but strangely beautiful landscape of mountains, moors and lochs, I had arrived in fishing paradise. It was all very much as I had imagined from the evocative writings of Bill Currie. To all intents and purposes, I behaved as if I owned the place. I fished where and when I wished. Perhaps a closer enquiry would have found some willing recipient of payment for my exploits but I found no real incentive to pursue such matters. It seemed a pretty alien concept to pay for the privilege of tramping the hills of my homeland when making such casual exploration of their waters. I think Alec would have been appalled at the notion of my doing otherwise. However, I did have a sense of responsibility regarding the issue of access. Had I met someone else in these remote parts, I would happily have deferred to their right of access and enjoyment of the place. After all, there was most certainly no limitation to the amount of water that could be fished. It would have seemed better to move on and fish another loch, preferably without ever having disturbed the other fisher. I also had an inherent regard for property in that I would never have used a boat without permission; there are those who see fit to boast of such a poor accomplishment. The small lochans did not, of course, have boats but some of the neighbouring, larger waters did, albeit most of these craft had seen much better days. Regrettably, it still seems to be the stamp of the Scottish Highlands that boats and boathouses – where they exist – are often in great disrepair. Of course, there are fine exceptions to this rule but, often, it seems that these accessories merely hint at the wealth and commitment of a bygone age.

In these earlier years, I rarely fished from a boat. On one occasion, I did make an exception and, in the company of a couple of fishing friends, hired a boat on one of the neighbouring larger waters. We were fishing in the first weeks of September on days when that glorious clear light of cooler and shortening days speaks of summer's end and the onset of autumn. The winds were high and we drifted the bays and shores with high expectation. The water was reputed to hold better than average fish for north-west Sutherland, hence our enthusiasm for its drifts. It was a shallow and very exposed loch – not that extensive – and, in the main, it proved to be quite dour. Hour by hour, we drifted its shores in the hope of hooking something exceptional. At the time, we were all quite young lads and 'exceptional' at this juncture would have been a brownie of over a pound – the magic weight that, for me at least, had been elusive. There was something compellingly hypnotic in the whole experience of perpetual drifting with eyes glued to the antics of the dashing bob fly hopping and skidding from trough to peak of the rolling waves. It all looked so enticing and, from my experience of the neighbouring middle lochan – I had yet to succeed on the upper of the three waters – there was a conviction that it was surely only a matter of time and the fly would be attacked explosively from below.

It was now late afternoon and we had drifted from shore to shore in high expectation. A shallow, drab and distant bar of flat moorland separated the angry rolling water from a cold blue sky above the Atlantic. When the offer came, it was a modest swirl that disturbed the wave – not at all explosive. I missed it, of course, and my companions had seen nothing of it. We were now all alert as I cast again from the drifting boat. Another definite swirl but again no contact was made. I had not experienced anything like this – I was used to the positively suicidal nature of the inhabitants of the middle lochan! At least one companion had spotted the take, so at least I could be credited with having moved something; it was not all make-believe! A third, tense and desperate cast somewhat to the front and right of the drifting boat, dropped the fly where I thought the trout to be. Once more, the swirl, the strike and – glory be – a plunging rod as line was ripped from my hands and off the reel! I remember the fight clearly as the fish staked its claim to freedom but I had played enough fish by this time to expect a successful outcome if I took my time and tired the fish before drawing it across the waiting net. It was a splendid trout of one pound four ounces; what a beauty! I was thrilled and so were my friends. We kept that trout and marvelled at its markings. It was a majestic enlargement of all that I had caught on the middle lochan, a large-scale version of all that had gone before. We fished on for another couple of hours and one of my friends had a strong pull from a further fish but it was not hooked. There was a sense of achievement in all of this. It was a sort of rite of passage from novice to competent angler. I had spent hours and days on different waters to get this far, as well as years of winter nights of fly-tying and great expectation. I had often wondered if I could handle the moment of hooking into something larger. And now, I knew. It was a wonderful affirmation that what

I had been doing previously was not all wrong. Deep down, I realised that my success was very much a case of being in the right place at the right time, of fishing with a small measure of competence, all seasoned with a very substantial measure of luck; such is fishing! A couple of days later, we returned to this loch and I got a splendid fish of one pound six ounces on the bob. I gave this trout to Alec and Maggie-Anne and there was a smile on their faces as I departed.

Over the years, I fished many other waters of the far north-west. I explored all of them with enthusiasm and high expectation. The thrill was in accessing waters in far-off places, often of stunning beauty. Some of these waters were visited because of their reputation, perhaps through an article read or a casual comment overheard. Others were visited following perusal of maps and sheer curiosity. Some were more productive than others. Sometimes, the arduous climb was unrewarded because the weather would turn foul on arrival and conditions were atrocious. On such occasions, the reputation of these waters had to remain uncertain. Others proved their worth in fairer weather.

One day, Alec proffered another gem of wisdom. For no reason in particular that I can recall, he made passing reference to a small dour loch by the roadside and how it could be worth a cast under certain conditions. I had seen this loch on many occasions and had noted occasional dimple rises in the flat calm of its surface on summer evenings. It was known to produce a small number of larger trout in the early season when the higher hill lochs were still in the grip of late winter or early spring at best. The size of these fish was reputedly good with trout of two pounds to be expected. I had even had an exploratory cast on this water in previous seasons but to no effect. As far as Alec was concerned, I had been there at the wrong time of year – much too late – and had fished in the wrong places and under the wrong conditions. He was extremely specific about where and when to fish this water. At his insistence, my future efforts were to be concentrated on the small grassy promontory marked by a line of wire fencing that came off the hill to the water's edge. I was to fish when the wind was steady and from the west and I was to start when the shine of the evening sun was first leaving the water. The preferred conditions all sounded ideal for fishing anywhere but why Alec, who was not a fisherman, should have been so specific about this loch, I do not know. However, in deference to his advice, I planned an assault when conditions were pretty much as he had described.

The loch in question is not large and it is very accessible. I suppose its position by the roadside held less attraction for me than more remote waters.

Crucially, there was a greatly increased likelihood of being challenged regarding a fishing permit in such an exposed corner by the roadside! Whatever, I recall putting my rod up and tying the usual proven cast of flies to a floating line with the warmth of the low summer sun setting on my back. The light changed subtly and I was ready to cast. With a soft steady westerly behind me, it was a relaxed cast that straightened my three flies in the gentle wave. This was indeed fly-fishing at its easiest. I would have been hard pressed to do anything other than present a true and straight line that gave good contact with those enticingly placed killer flies. And sure enough, the very first lengthened cast resulted in a great boil of a rise as a splendid trout rolled over the bob fly – my usual large and trusted Coch-Y-Bondhu. Now, by this time, I was well enough versed in the ways of trout and their rises to hold fire and relax on the strike. This was the sort of rise from a larger trout that required a mere firm but gentle raising of the rod and tightening of the line once the fish had rolled and gone down. And executing restraint is exactly what I did. To my surprise, on raising the rod, I felt nothing. Instead of a plunging rod and racing line, my flies were free and ready for the next cast. My blood was up! So, I had missed a sitter of a fish – a real banker and a good one at that. Now, I shall not bore you with the details of what followed. Suffice to say that in the next five minutes, I rose and missed as many trout – perhaps the same one on a couple of occasions. Whatever, they all came to the Coch-Y-Bondhu and I missed the lot. I could not believe it. How on earth could such perfect and easy rises be missed on so many occasions? I can still see the shining golden flanks of these fish, not one of them under a pound and a half in weight, the best well-in-excess of two pounds. Great red and black spots shone like beacons in the very last rays of the setting sun. But back to the depths they returned, leaving me frustrated and bewildered. And then, just as quickly as the window of opportunity had arisen, it disappeared. The sun was now completely off the water. The residual warmth seemed to disappear exceedingly quickly and the light wind that had seemed so welcome now breathed a cooler edge in the encroaching darkness. It all seemed so fitting to my mood as if some great orchestration was afoot to emphasise the drama, indeed tragedy, of the occasion. And that is how I left it. I took down my rod and left the place dispirited. Deep down, I knew that I had messed up a supreme opportunity. I might only have managed two or three fish but they would all have been real specimens from this north-west corner of Sutherland. These would have been fish to reinforce the splendid tradition of the place, my contribution to its reputation and romance but it was not to be.

The next morning, for want of anything better to do, I tidied my tackle bag. My mood had not lifted from one of irritation as I disconsolately sifted through nylon casts and flies. It was not improved when I noticed the broken point to the hook of an otherwise perfect bob fly that I had fished the night before. When did that happen? Did I not check the point on tying the cast? I thought I had. Did I hit a stone on the back cast? If so, I was not aware of it.

I have never returned to the dour loch. I had my chance and did not take it and, at least at the time, it seemed grossly inappropriate and almost inexcusable to try again. In a perverse way, this episode is one of my clearest and best-defined fishing memories. It seems strange that such a gripping memory should be one of such gross incompetence and failure. The veil had indeed been ripped momentarily but then very much restored in favour of the fish and good luck to them!

Despite other forays in the region, I was always drawn back to the small group of lochs on which I first started. It was here that I felt at home. They were not always easy to fish but sometimes they were exceedingly bountiful. When all is said and done, I suppose they came to define my enjoyment of trout fishing. I have visited them over a period of fifty years and they still enthral with the anticipation they afford and the very joy invoked by their continued exploration. There is always something new to be discovered either in the fish and in their catching or in some other facet of these wild places. I have visited them when conditions have been warm and conducive and the air has been heavy with the scent of bog myrtle. On such days, the light wind is welcome after the long scramble. I have also visited these waters when the wind has literally torn my clothes, tattering hems and cuffs. I have had the air swept from my lungs, so that breathing has been a painful gasp. There have been times when I have had to lean steeply into the gale, only to fall near senseless as the gust veered. Only with my face flattened against black peat and heather have I managed to relieve the suffocating choke in my chest. On this wild expanse of hills and moorland, I have wiped wind-drawn tears from my eyes and have lain in the low heather, gazing at the cold twinkling of thousands of stars. I have marvelled at the sweeps of misty white on deepest blue – great mysterious bands with racing trajectories that have shot into ragged heather fringes. And all the time the wind has raged, whipping water from the surface of the loch and throwing it violently on to the distant heather. On such awe-inspiring occasions, the catching of fish assumes a much lesser importance than that of merely being there – being part of the wild landscape and heritage of the place.

I could dwell further on the magnificence of north-west Sutherland but I have probably said enough to kindle memories in some fishers who can relate to my exploits. Hopefully, I may have fired the curiosity and imagination of at least some who do not know these parts. I have not been specific in naming the waters I have fished. You will find your own special places. Every summer when I had to leave this paradise, it was with a sense of regret. However, the short winter days would fly past and, with batches of newly-tied warriors to the ready, plans for the coming season would be made with renewed anticipation! The whole cycle was wonderfully addictive and, for years, seemed irreplaceable. However, over the years, other fishing inevitably came my way and, in recent times, deteriorating fitness has made the trek in these far hills more of an ordeal than a pleasure. So, my visits have been fewer. However, I can close my eyes and dream of the intimacy of these shores. I can see the lively peaty water glistening in the warmth of a summer afternoon and hear the waves lapping enticingly along the moorland shore. I have come to know something that has not changed in millennia. By chance, I have become part of a privileged tradition, something that is deeply satisfying to those who have been touched by its hand. It is something sacred; something to be cherished and something to pass on to others. If you do not know it, you will not miss it; if you have been anointed, it becomes part of your very being. Such is fishing in wild places. It is quite possible that I may never return to these early haunts, although I do have plans in the offing and feel in better shape for the rough trek than I have done for years! There is also an appointment – now fifty years overdue – with trout in a small roadside loch whose majestic ancestors I once so briefly encountered!

I shall close these wanderings by dreaming my way in fond memory on to the nearby sandy storm beach and scramble on to its rocky promontory. Its rose-red and grey rock is topped with grazed turf and flowers. In season, the pink thrift and blue hare bells replace the earlier flowering yellows of sedum and primrose and small patches of white, mountain avens. The whole cliff edge is alive with flowering plants vying for beauty with the meadowlands and its nearby twinkling burn. I am straining to hear the corncrake with its scratchy voice but it has long been absent. I look down from the rocky cliff into the blue-green water of the sandy bay and stare at steely shoals of summer salmon and vast shoals of glittering sand eels cruising the bay. Are they still there? Along the troughs of rolling breakers, I spot the frenzy of gulls, fulmars and gannets targeting the mackerel shoals and their prey. Do such shoals still exist or are they too something of the past? I am on the lookout for whales and seals.

I return to the golden-silver dunes and stop at the grassy cemetery with its weatherworn headstones. There, I kneel at the place where Alec and Maggie-Anne are laid to rest. My heart aches as I cry in solitude for these dear friends now departed. But my tears are also those of joy and gratitude for the love and affection of these lovely people – the love that should have been theirs for the child they never had. This is a lonely place. Here, children once laughed and played. Once, there were many, now they have all gone. As I stand again and face the Atlantic wind and sun, my tears are whipped from my face towards the distant hills and moorland now fast disappearing in a sweep of rain. As I turn, I have one last fleeting glimpse of sunlight caressing the distant rock above the small lochs. Then all is rapidly and fittingly shrouded in mist – the painful, yet joyous reality of all that has gone before in this most beautiful of places.

Drifts on Craggie

Some fishing spots have an attraction that, at best, only poorly can be defined. For me, Loch Craggie, near Lairg in Sutherland, is one such place. It is not particularly large, being little more than one mile in length and a quarter mile in width. Its banks are largely featureless and it has only one small island in its south-eastern corner. Its boathouse on the north-western promontory is in ruins; the very presence of its crumbling stonework and its once proud wooden beams with rusted corrugated roof speak of a long-past and more prosperous age. The round hill on its southern shore is glaringly unspectacular in comparison with the stunningly impressive mountains of north-west Sutherland; glimpses of these distant peaks makes for a stark and disconcerting contrast. The modest hill at Craggie has little in the way of redeeming features because, in light and uncertain winds, it makes mockery of intended drifts and casting efforts. I have seen casts tumble in astonishing fankles that presumably map the small vagaries of air pressure in the lee of this hill. Here I have seen a drifting boat spin on its long axis for apparently no reason whatsoever, yet again compromising fishing effort. In low water, the jumble of massive boulders that are barely concealed by its water surface can make Craggie a downright dangerous place to drift. Many a drift has come to a crunching halt on one of Craggie's hidden shallows! I stated that Craggie has only one island. This is true if one ignores the small incongruous raft of heather, grass and rushes with polystyrene base and anchor rope that is featured in the furthest bay of the north-west corner. To this list of far from positive features must be added the overwhelmingly large population of biting midges that frequent the normally sheltered mooring bay in Craggie's south-eastern corner. Count yourself fortunate if you have visited Craggie and not been demented by these ravenous hoards!

Given, the foregoing list of detractions, it may seem surprising that I should have visited Craggie on a regular basis for the past thirty years. In years gone by, I would fish this loch for a week-long stretch but, in more recent years, for only a couple of days at a time. This adds up to a lot of fishing on a water for which I have identified so many unappealing features. The explanation is to be found in the word 'mayfly'. Craggie is one of relatively few Scottish lochs in which phenomenal hatches of mayfly occur and, in this context, it is one of the best. Because of this, it is special and, for this reason, I continue to make the annual pilgrimage. As you get to know Craggie, you realise that is has many other notable redeeming features. Its long-wooded shore is teeming with nesting birds. I have seen otters and slow worms. You are greeted by the incessant calling of sandpipers at the sandy northern bay. Ospreys compete with your efforts at catching trout and sweeping kites bring life to the dour slopes of the hillside. Black-throated divers and their chicks explain the presence of the small artificial island. Orchids abound as the bluebells start to fade on the southern bank and the bright crimson beauty of marsh cinquefoil – and much more – startles as you first approach the boat. What more can you ask of your surroundings on a June morning?

I first visited Craggie at quite the wrong time. You generally must be high in the hills to get much return from trout fishing on a hot dry August day anywhere in Scotland and Craggie can hardly be classified as a high hill loch. I had been touring Sutherland on a camping holiday with my son David and, having had a great time catching an abundance of mostly smaller trout from a host of hill lochs, we ended up in Lairg with a boat on Craggie. There was a reasonable wave but the waters ahead of each drift glistened with an unrelenting blue. The scorching sun beat down on us and, not surprisingly, we struggled to catch more than the occasional trout. All of them were small and bore no resemblance to what I was anticipating from the enthusiastic writings of Bruce Sandison. This was disappointing because I had hoped to cap the week for David with something a bit out of the ordinary. By all accounts, Craggie should have been the place. Of course, I was being quite unrealistic. There are few places that would yield a better class of trout under such unfavourable conditions, at least using the traditional approach of near-surface flies that we practised. Perhaps a deeper fly, searching amongst the hulking boulders of Craggie would have been more productive but I find little enjoyment in the approach. A late evening cast with a small sedge, moth or midge pattern might have been worthwhile but we did not have that opportunity. I left Craggie more intrigued than disillusioned. It was surely a place that merited a return visit at a potentially more productive time of year.

The return visit was to be several years later and, importantly, during the second half of June. By this time, David was in his early teens and showing all the signs of the burgeoning independence of his peers. Crucially, his approach to fishing was not to be limited to any perceived wisdom of his father. If there was an alternative approach to exploring the catching of trout, David would explore it. We were accompanied by my younger son Euan who had scarcely hit the teen barrier. (Here I must apologise to my daughter Eilidh who was not included on this trip: Eilidh, I still think you were too young and anyway, despite your protests to the contrary, I think the trips with your mum to Edinburgh's Chamber Street Museum cannot have been all bad. Forgive me if I am wrong!)

I have never kept a fishing diary because I find it somewhat pedantic to list numbers and sizes of trout, flies on which they were caught and diverse weather conditions. Others will disagree and, no doubt with some justification, see some merit in the keeping of records. I prefer a more relaxed approach to anything resembling success with trout. Over the years, you accumulate a host of experiences and memories out of which an intuition is distilled regarding good and perhaps not so good conditions. At best, this feeling for things might temper your enthusiasm for venturing forth if prevailing conditions do not fall into the most favourable category. However, in my experience, opportunity is often the most decisive factor that determines when I am on the water and, if I am out at all, the last thing I need is diminished enthusiasm. Fishing can be difficult enough without believing I am not going to catch anything! So, without a detailed record, I can only paint a broad-brush approach to any success that my sons and I had on Craggie at mayfly time.

It all started on the first morning of our week when we found the windward fringes of the loch littered with the amazingly large shucks of hatched mayfly. We saw hundreds of them; I suspect thousands must have hatched. These shucks must have been the outer 'clothing' of hatches from previous days – the remnants of the final larval stages that progress over a two-year period – because, on the morning in question, there was no indication of surface activity by feeding trout or hatching mayfly. This was to prove typical of early mornings on subsequent days. Then, as the sun shone and the morning got warmer, a change suddenly appeared on the water. It was almost as if a switch had been thrown – an analogy that is probably a reasonable way of describing the triggers that affect the very biology of hatching. And what a change it was! Where once the surface had appeared devoid of insects and fish, the whole surface of the loch started to heave and boil with rising fish. It was easy to see what lay behind this frenzy because, across the water small 'sail ships' would suddenly appear, flutter and spin on the surface for a second or two and then suddenly disappear in a swirling boil. What a sight! The rise was hardly continuous but it occurred in bouts of varying intensity throughout the late morning and afternoon. At times, it reached fever pitch with trout boiling intensely across the bays. At other times, although the weather did not appear to have changed, things went quiet. Then, for no apparent reason, the hectic surface activity was resumed. What an opportunity for catching surface-feeding fish! Such was the pattern that was repeated throughout our week.

I had heard about the Craggie mayfly and, before the trip started, had bought some dressings that I hoped might be useful. These were large, mostly olive, fan-wing dressings and, when there was a reasonable wave on the water, they did well. Occasionally, they succeeded in fooling fish in calmer conditions. We fished them dry with occasional tweaks on the surface (always a good option) or as tripping dapped flies. Invariably, the dapped fly would induce many takes – often more than one from the same fish – as the fly bounced and skittered from wave to wave. Dapping is tremendously effective at bringing fish to the fly – and what a joy it is to see the repeated shining gold flanks of a good fish – but the success rate at hooking and landing such fish can be low. The takes to a more stationary dry fly – with the occasional tweak – seem to be more certain; more fish are securely hooked and landed than on the dapped fly.

Once the fish started rising, it was relatively easy to spot the feeding grounds, associated with the hatch. From a distance, the wheeling gulls and (formerly) terns were a good indicator of hatching fly. Most activity seemed to be confined to the two bays at the more northerly end of the loch, with some definite hot spots. The drift between the two points of rocky shallows defining the mouth of the larger bay was always good; anywhere amidst the shallow tumble of rocks and sand in the smaller bay was a banker. Drifts along the long rocky shore could yield some very good fish.

It was a joy to fish Craggie when the mayfly was hatching. Over the years, its bounty may very well have resulted in my fishing this loch to the exclusion of many other productive and enticing waters. It became something of a family affair because it was here that my sons mastered most of what they know about fly fishing for trout. It was not always easy. There were tough times when the wind would suddenly blow hard and the drifts became rough and, on reflection, dangerous. I suppose I took a somewhat cavalier approach to boat safety but, at that time, health and safety issues had not assumed any great importance amongst the fishing fraternity. At the time, you learned to respect the weather, the water, the boat and the capabilities of your companions and you then behaved accordingly. I always try to have everything in place in the boat: the drogue, the net, the priest, the weighing scales, the bag for trout and much more – all have their place; there should be nothing lying loose that clutters the boat or that is likely to be dislodged and come clattering down in the gunnels. All this may sound like common sense but it takes a lot of organising and experience to get it right. No doubt, some of my companions find me over-pedantic in these matters but I do hope they find that any order in my ways pays dividends. I have always discouraged rods from standing when fishing for trout from a boat, partly from a safety perspective and partly because of the inevitable disturbance that a higher profile presents to feeding trout. If you avoid disturbance and remain seated, it is quite astonishing how close to a drifting boat trout will rise in an apparently undisturbed manner. Fishing a shorter line allows you to discern the type of rise and that, for me at any rate, results in a higher proportion of fish hooked and landed. I have caught innumerable trout – and good ones at that – within yards of the boat. I have even had good Craggie fish leap into the boat as they pursued natural flies! Interestingly, any short-line success has often been at its best when I have been fishing on my own. There is something inevitable about this in that the probability of inadvertent boat disturbance is likely to be reduced. I hate line splash and boats that rock with undue casting effort and I think the trout share my dislike. This poses something of a dilemma in that, for me, boat fishing for trout is very much a social occasion. I have loved every day on the water in the company of my sons and indeed others, despite anything they may have deduced to the contrary from all my moaning and groaning at missed fish and assorted mishaps! But, if I want to up my own rod catches in terms of number and size of trout, then I should probably fish alone. It is only then that I can be selective in terms of which fish to cover and how, in an uncompromised mode, to best present the fly. I remember one season on Craggie when, after a disappointing week – at least in terms of number and size of fish caught when fishing with my sons – I sneaked back again on my own a couple of weeks later. At the start of my first drift in the smaller bay, I very quietly eased the boat into the bank and started to lengthen the dapping line. I took a tremendous amount of care to avoid all boat noise and – I like to think consequently – a good trout took me confidently within yards of the boat in the essentially calm water of the leeward shore. It was an absolute cracker of a fish that weighed just short of two pounds. I would not have caught that fish had I been sharing the boat because there would not have been enough room for two rods to start an undisturbed drift at that spot. So, it is very much a case of 'horses for courses'. If I want to get (perhaps, selfishly) the best return to my own rod, then I am probably best to fish alone from the boat. If I want a good-fun day on the water with lots of banter and plenty of fish coming to the boat, then I shall most happily fish with company. An alternative would be to take turns on the oars, maximising the fishing prospect of one rod at a time. Perhaps it is surprising that my companions and I do not do this more often.

There is no doubt in my mind that the quality of fishing in Craggie was higher when my sons and I started than it has been in recent years. I am thinking here in terms of numbers of larger fish in a typical catch. I do not think there is necessarily anything sinister in this trend. I have seen so many lochs decline and improve over the years that I feel inclined to assert that most, if not all, lochs are subject to shifts in population demography. In most Scottish lochs, limited food supply and variable recruitment through spawning are likely to be key determinants of population structure (number and size of trout in different age classes). Longevity may be less important; trout will not necessarily live to a greater age in waters with good feeding although, where recruitment is not excessive, they may well grow to a considerably greater size. For years, our typical Craggie basket would contain several fish just short of two pounds; fish of one pound eleven-, twelve- or thirteen ounces were common. A good daily basket of fish kept would be in the order of ten fish with a total weight of twelve or thirteen pounds and at least a couple of these fish would be just short of the two-pound mark. By any standards, this is good wild trout fishing in Scotland. There are other un-stocked lochs in Scotland that can match these totals but they (mostly) do not feature a mayfly hatch. I am sure other rods would do better than ourselves. We were, when all is said and done, still honing our skills but we did catch fish! The largest we caught was a fish of well over three pounds but it fought poorly and should have weighed more for its length. I have heard of a fish of four pounds being caught and suspect that was amongst the largest in the loch. In recent years, smaller fish have become more prevalent and, at least for me, the catching of larger fish, for which Craggie was renowned, has become something of a rarity. I suspect that there may have been a succession of years favourable to good spawning and juvenile survival and that, in recent years, the loch may have been overstocked if size of fish is a preferred index. It may also be relevant that, in my experience, the mayfly hatches of recent years do not approach those of previous seasons. Perhaps more fish and a limited food supply are pushing Craggie in the direction of most Scottish lochs. Some big fish are still caught and, of course, things can change for the better. It would be wonderful to return to the days of plenty with free-rising fish of quality, gorging themselves on an abundance of mayfly. I see no reason why, in the course of time, this should not be the case. I suspect that all that is required are a few years of poor spawning and reduced juvenile survival.

I may have given the impression that fishing at mayfly time was always easy. Occasionally, it did appear to be relatively straightforward and a reasonably presented fly amongst rising trout would do the business. However, at other times the whole game could be enormously frustrating. I once spent an early evening fishing the smaller bay surrounded by rising fish. I could cover fish without the slightest problem but they steadfastly refused my fly. I changed the fly on umpteen occasions and tried all the proven dressings that had worked on previous days, weeks and seasons, all to no avail. I knew the fish were feeding on hatching mayfly but I just could not connect. With hindsight, I suspect that the rise was to flies in the transition between larval stage and dun and that all of my offerings may have been riding too high in the water. If I encounter this again, I shall have no hesitation in stripping down and messing up a few flies in the hope that they will drown in the surface film. The whole experience was enormously frustrating but, at the same time, intriguing. The next morning saw things return to normal with readily taking fish but neither the intensity of rise nor quality of fish matched that of the previous evening. I have only twice seen an intensity of rising fish to match that of Craggie on that evening. Both instances were on Sutherland lochs on hot August days and both were in response to a sudden fall of flying red ants. I suspect that nearly every fish in these two lochs must have switched to surface feeding; for a couple of hours, both waters were absolutely heaving with rising fish, of whose number and quality I had previously been unaware. On those occasions, I caught some splendid fish – what an 'eye-opener'!

I mentioned that fan-wing dressings could be effective; they always have done well for us and I am sure they will continue to do so. As you drift across Craggie, you become aware of two distinct sizes of hatched fly. These size classes may represent two distinct species of mayfly. Both sizes can be found on the water at the same time and I am unaware of the trout showing any preference for one size over the other. When the water is calm or showing only a slight ripple, I have probably caught more fish on a smaller dressing. However, I doubt if this reflects any size preference for the natural on the part of the trout. I suspect that the larger artificial is simply less convincing as a food item when the trout can inspect it closely in undisturbed water. In rough water with bigger waves, I prefer a larger fly, simply because I can see it more clearly. So: small waves, small flies; big wave, big flies. Over the years, it has become apparent that, even when bedraggled and shredded by encounters with trout, some of these fan-wings remain irresistible and continue to be top catchers of fish. I still have one fly (smaller size) that has been with us for over thirty years; that is a long time for a fly that has been used every year! It lost its wings (although there are still a couple of original wing fibres) after a couple of seasons. However, it continued to catch fish and so was retained. Eventually, it lost most of its tail and then most of its olive body and hackle. It still caught fish and so it survived the annual purge when other, apparently useless, flies were binned. David and I used to fight over this fly because it most definitely seemed to be a winner. It never got physical but there was a distinct feeling of being disadvantaged when another rod fished this fly and you were left to select an alternative from hundreds of other languishing candidates. They all looked good but, for some reason, seemed to lack that special 'something' that made the tattered fly so successful. Of course, I stripped a host of other flies to the bare bone hoping to match the heroic warrior but nothing ever quite did the trick. I hoped that repeated skirmishes with trout teeth might produce some compatriots from amongst its peers but, although we now have plenty of dowdy flies, they all seem to lack that special trigger. Several years ago, I took pity on the 'special one' and gave it a makeover. It was still catching fish and therefore continued to give confidence but it was nearly impossible to see its sorry form on all but the calmest of waters. One early morning, as I sat contemplating this fly, I decided to refurbish it. I reasoned that, if the renovated fly should no longer catch fish, then I could always strip it back again to its bare successful minimum. It was furnished with one additional fibre in the tail and (having no olive hackles to hand) a short-grizzled hackle at its neck. I secured the tail and neck fibres with red tying silk because I did not have any black silk to match the original tying. It got its first outing that same morning and immediately did the business. If anything, it was now more deadly than before! In recent years, I have looked at this shambles of a fly and have seriously considered further renovation. However, I think I should now leave well alone and concentrate on getting other flies into an appropriately dishevelled state. I would hate to lose this fly because of all the memories it engenders. It has become something of a treasure and perhaps it should be removed from active service. One more season perhaps?

Other dressings have, of course, had their moments. We have had good success (sometimes spectacularly so) with Grey-Wulff and Yellow-Wulff dressings. These flies look incongruous but, with their somewhat forward leaning split wings, they seem to be good deceivers of trout, especially in a reasonable wave. I have tried all sorts of emerger patterns and some have, on occasion, proved good but not better than my bedraggled fan-wings. The only other dressing that I would wish to have in my box is anything that approximates the mayfly spinner. This ultimate stage of a mayfly's life can be deadly. I always fish it in spent form, so I am looking for something sparse; anything with flattened hackle wings, a few tail fibres and a light-coloured body with dark ribbing is good. There are evenings when the fish switch on to these offerings and, for a short while, the sport can be fast and furious. However, this occurrence is sporadic and, unlike the daytime hatch of duns in warm weather, does not always happen. Generally, I have found that, as darkness approaches, the fishing fades with the light. I have found it more profitable to go home and rest in readiness for the excitement of a new day than to persevere into the dusk. This, of course, applies to mayfly time when there are plenty of opportunities to be had with big daytime feeders when the hatch is on.

I know that I am set in my ways when it comes to fishing Craggie anytime during the mayfly hatches of June and the first part of July. Invariably, I shall be pursuing rising fish with some sort of dry fly. This is not necessarily a good thing in terms of fish caught. One of the most beautiful baskets of fish that I have seen from Craggie fell to another boat in mid-July. I had little success that day with my usual tactics but here was an angler who had tried something different. His splendid bag of trout had fallen for a small sedge dressing. I do not recall seeing sedges on the water and, if they were there, I had certainly ignored their potential, preferring to pursue my usual approach with mayflies. I also know that on other occasions a small Black Gnat fished dry can do very well, even when the fish are apparently taking hatching mayfly. I do not suppose that there is much surprise in this; small black flies can often do well. I think it was my son David who first abandoned the usual mayflies because he could see numerous small midge-like flies on the water. He delved into one of my fly boxes and attached a very small Black Gnat to match what was on the water. The trout loved it! On the day in question, I remember having to abandon the boat to spend some time with Euan away from the water. Our intention was to return and, when we did so some two hours later, David was full of the excitement of trout missed and trout caught! He had eased the boat into the margins of the small bay and was sight fishing with the small black fly for rising trout. He had plenty to recount having just played and lost a fish in the two-pound class and then landing one just short of that mark. What good invention and what great fishing! I was truly pleased for him.

Both of my boys developed their skills at boat fishing on Craggie. I suppose things initially were easier for David because he was that bit older but Euan also did well. He would studiously unravel any tangles in his line (as did David) and then recommence his fishing. I remember a period when Euan repeatedly lost some better fish. His rod would be well bent taking the strain of a good fish but his line management did not quite meet the requirement of maintaining contact when a bigger fish would run hard towards (and often under) the boat. He just seemed to be losing too many big fish and I became concerned that he might become disheartened. One afternoon when the rise was on, we were drifting across weed beds just south of the smaller bay when Euan hooked something good. I gave all the usual parental encouragement about maintaining contact and hand-lining if necessary should the fish run at the boat. Things were going well but I was anxious and keen that yet another fish should not be lost to his rod. After a couple of minutes, I decided to ease the boat into a tiny sandy spit on the shore in the hope that I might divert any untoward incident should the fish run at the boat. It was with an enormous sense of relief and elation that I netted that fish for Euan. I think it weighed one pound eleven ounces. He was delighted and so was I. I felt he had come of age as a trout fisherman. It is moments like this that are my clearest memories of Craggie and perhaps, in the end, it is memories such as these that matter to me more than any others.

The years have gone by on Craggie and, given their other commitments, it is now difficult for me to arrange trips with my sons. I hope we can sometime manage a trip down memory lane and drift Craggie together! I remember once meeting a man who was then very much my senior who was out fishing Craggie with his then elderly father. The older man needed help to and from the boat so he was struggling a bit physically. They were only on the water for a short afternoon but returned with a beautiful trout weighing more than two pounds caught on a frighteningly large Blue Zulu. I suspect it may have been the older man's last day on the water and if so, I hope he enjoyed it. Even if it is not my last trip, I would love to do something similar with my sons. I also hope to fish Craggie with my daughter Eilidh. She was once with me on a neighbouring loch and enjoyed herself. Emotionally, Eilidh and I are very close although we now live on different sides of the globe, I hope one day she will join me and understand something of why fishing has been such a large part of my life. However, I have a sneaking feeling that any such future trips will involve grandchildren and all the challenges they will pose. I look forward to that immensely!

Nothing in this world remains constant and fishing waters are certainly no exception. Craggie has had a dip in fortunes, at least in terms of fish size. As discussed earlier, I fully expect this may be reversed in due course. What cannot be reversed is the passing of people with the passing of time. I got all my fishing on Craggie through the agency of David and Margaret Walker in Lairg. A few years ago, David took ill and rather suddenly passed away. When I last spoke to Margaret, she too was suffering from poor health and was looking to pass on the fishing rights. For years, my sons and I stayed at the Lairg caravan site run by Margaret and Lewis. Sadly, Margaret has also passed away and it will be a tough call for Lewis and his son Alastair to keep things going; to this end, I wish them well. Whatever, I hope Craggie will remain a quality wild-trout fishery, open to the vagaries of weather and seasonal change and open to those who relish the challenge and excitement of encountering Scottish trout fishing with mayfly at its very best.

Mostly About Floats

There is something about the fascination of perch fishing that has stayed with me through thick and thin. I started early but not as early as some and, although I have whiled away many a hot summer day in pursuit of perch, I have never made a truly concerted effort to master the intricacies of their capture under the myriad of conditions that might be encountered. I have been inadvertently selective in when I have fished for perch and have nearly always found myself by the water under conditions of relative warmth and calm. For me, hot summer days go hand in hand with perch fishing. Perch have enthused me at different times. They have always been there should I turn to them and, for that reason, my appreciation of their pursuit has persisted, if somewhat sporadically. But there is something deeply attractive in their capture that has made them special. In the main, my perch fishing over the years has meant float fishing and, for me, there is something about this approach that is quintessential to all angling; a responsive float, being the visual communicator of contact between fisher and fish, represents the epitome of what angling is all about. It is the early warning system of impending action, the wake-up call to attentiveness and high anticipation of what is happening in the depths of a hidden world. There are other thrills in angling, not least the visual excitement of takes to the dry fly, the steady draw of a turning salmon or the determined knock and running of line to a fished worm. But there is something distinctly special about watching and interpreting the surface movement of a float and its subsequent disappearance. It sort of marks the line of contact between fisher and fish, the very essence of ripping the veil. Hours of float fishing on a hot summer's day can become downright hypnotic where the float is essentially stared into invisibility. The whole phenomenon (when in pursuit of carp) has been most evocatively compared by Arthur Ransome in *Rod and Line* to that of taut nerves and hallucinations that imbues De Quincey's *Confessions of an Opium Eater*. You have been warned!

I have caught perch by other means – worming with paternoster or ledger tackle or, occasionally, by spinning. The first perch I caught was from Duddingston Loch – that attractive wildlife haven in the city of Edinburgh. This city is blessed with many green areas with plenty of water. I am sure that most Edinburgh residents – I was once one myself – do not appreciate to the full their natural heritage. This is a heritage that was part planned, part incidental. To live in Edinburgh is to live within walking distance of trout streams and small still waters populated by perch, roach and pike. Duddingston Loch is one such water and, at the time I fished, it had a limited extent of shore that was open to anglers. There were a few hundred yards of shoreline from the jetty wall to Hangman's Rock – what an intriguing name – that was available to the fishing public. Most evenings during the summer months would see a few keen souls plying their art along this stretch. Most were after perch, some were seeking pike. Most were bait fishing, some were spinning. Some were young and some were old. Some were experienced and some were novices. I belonged to the category of young, novice, bait-fisher for perch.

I recall having read about how to assemble a basic paternoster tackle and that is essentially what I fished. My first outing was on one fine summer's evening when I cycled through Holyrood Park and took my place on the jetty. There were one or two other anglers but I do not remember anyone having any success. What I do remember was that, as the evening progressed and darkness encroached, I reeled in my bait slowly and contemplatively thinking of a fruitless evening, at least in terms of fish caught. And then, I got that all-important knock and tug that registers a taking fish. I caught two perch that evening and learnt the importance of fishing a moving bait for this most predatory of fish. No doubt, perch can be caught on stationary baits but a moving bait seems to trigger their aggressive response and results in a lot more fish being caught. These were not big perch but, at the time, that did not matter. I remember taking them home and grilling them for my parents' breakfast. If they did not relish this delicacy, then they were too polite to say so. Years later, when I lived in Sweden, I learnt that juniper-smoked perch ranks amongst the most relished of fish cuisine in Scandinavia. Well-prepared with herbs, it is truly delicious!

Perch are known to tolerate much lower oxygen concentrations in water than do members of the salmon family. I recall trout kills at low summer levels on the River Tweed when perch were surviving in the tepid waters of Duddingston Loch. Mortality on the Tweed was at night when oxygen levels would plummet as plants competed with fish for available oxygen. The problem was less during the daytime when plants contributed to the oxygenation. However, if conditions became severe, there would even be perch kills at Duddingston and no fishing was allowed.

As the years went by, I fished elsewhere for perch. I recall sorties to the muddy flats at the top of Loch Venachar. This was dangerous and awkward fishing where I caught more trout on the spinner than I did perch! There was also a loch near Galashiels where smallish perch would readily take a float-fished worm. The floated worm was cast from the tree-lined bank and allowed to drift along the shoreline in the wind. Again, it was the movement that seemed most critical and resulted in most fish. The fish with their tiger-stripes could be seen readily in the water and it was an education in fish behaviour to watch their reaction to the worm. In the end, there was always one willing victim that opted for attack as a preferred strategy regarding an intrusive worm.

But my big success with perch lay elsewhere. Loch Gelly was a medium-sized water in Fife and it had a reputation for winter pike and summer perch. I read about it in a useful booklet on coarse fishing in Scotland. At the time, there were many dedicated coarse fishers in Scotland who knew their waters well but, overall, coarse fishing was pretty much discounted by most Scottish anglers. This reflected the abundance of available trout fishing, much of which was available at very reasonable prices through local angling clubs. If you lived in the Borders of Scotland or the Clyde valley, you fished for trout. It was all part of the tradition and expectation. To fish for other species would have been to enter relatively unknown territory, often without the help of local mentors. There were, of course, always exceptions and the ardent few who focussed on coarse fish no doubt did well. There used to be fine and helpful – often intriguing – articles in the angling press, pertaining to coarse fishing, such as those pertaining to the excellent roach fishing in the tidal waters of the Tay at Perth or bream fishing at Lochmaben in south-west Scotland. However, the further north you travelled, the less likely you were to encounter lochs with anything other than salmonids. This meant that the wealth of coarse fishing in Scotland, although cherished by a healthy minority, went largely unacknowledged by most Scottish freshwater anglers. For those that did know about it, however, there were some real gems of opportunity to be had. For those in the know, Loch Gelly was one such water, a place where better than average fish could be caught.

It proved relatively easy to catch good perch in Loch Gelly. It was possibly mostly a case of knowing where the bigger fish were to be found that led to their successful capture, rather than anything intrinsically clever in the methods used. I do not recall spending much fruitless time here and probably fortuitously stumbled on some of the better feeding patches. The best that I found was the reed-fringed bank towards the far end of the loch on the opposite side to the shore with its scattering of pines. Here, when the wind blew strong and steady and when the sun shone brightly, you could drift a float above a large lobworm and let it work in the wave. It could be a most killing method. The tip of the float would bob brightly in the wind and progress like a boat in distress until it most suddenly would bob then disappear abruptly in a series of stabbing jerks as the fished moved off with the bait. It was then a case of tightening into the predator and bringing the lively captive to the net. The fight was short but strong with determined tugging runs in the shallow water. I used to fish with a length of 4-lb nylon on my fly reel and line and, on my trout fly rod, the fish would often pull line off the reel as it sought refuge. The fish were invariably about one and a quarter pounds in weight. On a good afternoon, four or five fish might be taken.

I believe things have changed at Loch Gelly. When I stopped fishing its shores, there was talk of a rainbow trout fishery. This seemed inappropriate given the nature of the loch as a quality coarse fishery. But such developments had taken place elsewhere in the neighbourhood so it came as no great surprise that it was being mooted. Recent inspection of relevant websites indicates a current controversy as to 'who, where and when' regarding fishing on Loch Gelly. I am pleased to have fished it when I did.

Stopping fishing at Loch Gelly coincided with moving to Scandinavia. The Upland region of eastern Sweden is a low-lying land of inland lakes and Baltic coast. Its inland waters are populated by coarse fish such as pike, perch, bream and roach. The coastal Baltic is similar with, at the time, the bonus of seasonal herring, cod and Baltic salmon and sea trout. It was from the rounded, weathered rocks of Swedish lakesides that my children first caught fish. We fished with simple extending rods of cheap graphite to which red and white polystyrene floats and silver hooks were attached with strong nylon. The tackle resembled the most primitive and inexpensive of 'roach poles' that could be bought just about anywhere across the huge land mass of a hot Swedish summer. These were happy days when the only concern was to ensure the family had some very basic feel for what they were doing, coupled to a sense of respect for the environment and hazards of our local water. We learned how to catch better bream and shared the thrill of feeling the weight of these fish on light tackle. It was all pretty idyllic and I took great pleasure in sharing the enthusiasm of the youngsters in pursuing these fish. Many a hot afternoon would fade into the twilight of a late Swedish summer evening before hosts of whining biting mosquitoes would send us packing. Despite the mosquitoes, very happy times indeed!

Whatever joy I got out of catching coarse fish on float tackle, my main enthusiasm for the approach lay in the pursuit of that 'in-between' fish, the grayling. This fish is classified amongst the salmonids because of its adipose fin, that small structure lying between the dorsal and tailfins. However, in much of its behaviour and indeed appearance, the grayling is quite similar to coarse fish such as roach and dace. For me, its main attraction as a sport fish lay in its feeding behaviour in the winter months of river systems where I fished for trout in season. At the turn of the year when trout were spawning and out of season, the grayling would be feeding avidly – at least in spells – and this provided the excuse for winter excursions and a different perspective of the river from that of spring and summer. Not all rivers hold grayling; in fact, remarkably few do so. They need clean, well-oxygenated water with good access to more sedately flowing reaches than are normally found in typical Scottish torrents. They are more a fish of the lowlands than the highlands.

So, a typical grayling day would always find me in some secluded and pastoral environment. And what a joy it was to be out on the river in the winter months! The days were short and I would often only fish for an afternoon and into the encroaching dusk. My first serious sortie in pursuit of grayling was at the turn of the year with my friend Les. We were on the Lyne water, a small tributary of the Tweed and we were fishing in the neighbourhood of the small village of Romano Bridge. I have absolutely no recollection of why we ended up in Romano Bridge (there was a pub) but I suspect Les would have read about the Lyne somewhere and may possibly already have given it a try. What I do know is that any merits of our approach were attributable to Les and not myself. Somewhere along the line, he had got hold of a copy of Reg Righyni's book on grayling. This small volume proved to be both informative and inspirational on how to catch these fish, not least in how to use float tackle in their pursuit. We were enthused and, as naive but aspiring disciples of the Righyni approach, we got stuck into matters with uncompromising zeal. Les got us making floats from balsa wood and piano-string wire. Apparently, nothing available 'off the shelf' was of any use. We fashioned the floats with scalpels and whipped nylon loops to the inserted wire. Coats of white undercoat and fluorescent yellow or red paint were studiously applied and subsequently varnished. We were truly proud of our creations and I am sure we basked in the assumed approval of Righyni. We may well have ended up with floats very like those that could be bought in many tackle shops south of the border but, in truth, they were probably not available in Scotland at the time. At least, given the effort that went into their construction, I like to think that was the case! And, of course, if I was to go grayling fishing today, I would start by shunning all that is available to buy and start, as before, by making my own floats. On a more serious note, Righyni got it right. His prescription for grayling floats was first rate both in terms of visibility and sensitivity on the rivers we fished.

Preparations did not stop with floats. Les insisted on the stealthy excavation of compost heaps around the land. We were after small pink worms (not always brandlings with their yellow stripes). My father's garden was a favourite spot. We seemed to have an excessive profusion of small eating pears from an old tree and these – the damaged ones – when spread on the compost heap, provided the most alluring substrate for small pink worms. We would dig them up and stuff them into small hessian bags that we had carefully sewed. The bags leaked worms everywhere! I am not sure that I ever returned to Les his father's garden spade. For years, it remained at my place and my father was forever on at me to return it to its rightful owner. We just did not seem to have much time for such matters having just started the untold hardships (having to get out of bed) that still confront university students. (If you want the spade as a memento Les, I shall have a good rummage through my plethora of gardening equipment to see if it can be found. However, I suspect it may have graduated to the realms of saleroom auction.) Surprisingly, Les and I also graduated from university and, perhaps more surprisingly, our ways were to part for some thirty-plus years. We eventually did meet up again and fishing today would be seriously lacking without the enthusiasms and escapades we share – but that is another story.

Rods and reels were very basic and not very appropriate. I think Rhygini might have shaken his head but I like to think that he might have sympathised in that we made do with what we could afford. The saving grace was that we often fished small waters with much shorter 'trots' between rod and float than Rhygini might have practised on most of his rivers. I initially used the short spinning rod and reel that I inherited from Sandy but I soon purchased a longer 'coarse' rod.

On reflection, it was far too cumbersome and slow in action but it mostly proved adequate. So there we were, intrepid grayling fishermen both, accompanied on many occasions by assorted partners in crime, all set to explore and master what the winter months might offer.

The first excursion to the Lyne was a typical winter's day with frost slowly dissipating as the day warmed. The coldness never quite left the riverbank and, as darkness approached, the chill increased. We caught a few grayling that day. They were mostly small but I did get one fish that was much more substantial than the others. Typical of many lager fish on the Lyne, it was darker in colour than its smaller brethren. It weighed about one pound four ounces and was to prove, as the years unfolded, to be something of a specimen for the Lyne. No doubt, there are larger specimen grayling in the Lyne but, although I caught numerous good fish, I never took a larger grayling from the stretch at Romano Bridge. We both enthused over its capture and relived its capture as we sought warmth over a pint by the fire of the village pub. It was a pretty bleak watering hole but that did not matter at the time. I made many further short outings to that stretch on the Lyne. It was not a water that could accommodate intensive and prolonged rod pressure. I suspect that its grayling may have been somewhat nomadic and may have wandered upstream from the Tweed. I think this may be true of other smaller Tweed tributaries in which grayling were to be found. I assume larger tributaries like the Teviot would have a more substantial resident stock. From subsequent trips, it became apparent that the run from which I took that first larger grayling was not a particularly favoured pool. I tried it on many other occasions but had barely any success. On the other hand, I found stretches that were consistently good. A favourite run was that adjacent to the road and below the neighbouring house gardens. It featured some bankside bushes and fish would lie tight in against – perhaps under – their branches. A quiet, delicate approach was required if the fish were not to be scared. On most days, a couple of good fish was the norm before the lie was unduly disturbed by the commotion of hooked fish. Other streams and pools were apparently less favoured by grayling. Occasionally, we found trout hot spots which we learnt to avoid.

Progressively, we switched our attentions from the Lyne to the Leader at Earlston. As before, we fished worm tails on very small hooks, repeatedly varying the shotting and fishing depth in relation to the streams we fished. This was a lovely stretch of water from which we consistently took good bags of fish, with the best fish weighing more than two pounds. As on the Lyne, there were streams and pools that proved to be consistently good; others much less so. It was by trial and error that we got to grips with the hot spots and could concentrate our efforts accordingly. There was one particularly good pool below the iron footbridge down from the monastery. Beneath the bridge, the river bottom was sandy and a careful approach here could result in a good bag of fish, mostly taken below the rod tip. Some of these fish were of very good weight and none of them were small. The approach to this pool along the rounded surface of a brick culvert is one of the very few places where I have executed a good fall into a river. This resulted in waders full of very cold water. By the end of the day, it was very difficult to remove my boots. My trouser legs were frozen and had to be prised from the inside of my waders. Exactly what happened to my legs, I shudder to think! This was also the stream from which Les and I scrambled up a steep banking on the way to our next pool. We were intent on taking a short cut and this necessitated a brief visit to the precincts of the monastery. The way was steep and tough being covered in brambles and rhododendron. As we emerged from this tangle-wood uttering a string of expletives, we were confronted by a monk. When I say confronted, I mean he was seated in silence some two yards from our point of exit. I swear he did not bat an eyelid but I think we were both a bit embarrassed and did not stop to discuss the matter! Even today, it is difficult to know what could meaningfully have been said in this surreal encounter.

The last stretch as the river approached its confluence with the Tweed was also good but this was bailiff territory and we were generally given short shrift! Our other favourite pool was above the bridge in the village itself. On occasion, this stream seemed to be full of grayling and they were often keen to take the worm. We often fished here at last light and strained to see the float in the encroaching darkness. Nothing daunted, I tried making a float with a small LED tip and minute battery so that we could fish in the dark. The idea was good and I did get some fish in very poor light. But I never quite got the buoyancy right and the LED float lacked sensitivity. I wish now that I had pursued this idea; it is intriguing to think of fish being caught well into the dark. I think we mostly stopped fishing because of poor light long before the grayling stopped feeding.

These were wonderful days of shared pleasure. For Les and others, they spilled over into days on the Teviot where some real crackers were caught. I never got into this and continued my efforts on Lyne and Leader until my move to Sweden brought to an end my grayling sojourn. In dry weather, the sloping banks across frosted fields at the start of each day would be glistening in the morning sun and would lead to purposeful waters. These flowed cold and serene, washed clear of all weed and leaf fall from the autumn floods. It was magic to tramp the banks waiting to see the inevitable arrogant heron on one corner and, at the next bend, the usual spent salmon, always in the same spot and always disturbed by our wade. The cold air meant that our rod rings would freeze up, necessitating thawing with hacked fingers in the cold. This occurred with increasing frequency and decreasing effect as the light faded and another good day would come to an end. We would stumble contentedly those last few yards in the encroaching darkness, past the badger sett below the layby above Sorrowless field – a beguiling name that seemed appropriate to our mood.

I stopped grayling fishing in the Borders of Scotland because I left for Sweden and, regrettably, I may never get back into this world of grayling, floats and worm tails. (Sweden, incidentally, has marvellous grayling fishing but, because of other commitments, I never pursued it.) It was a magic world to frequent when I did but I suspect it is a thing of the past. I am sure it is possible to now buy permits to fish what was once an unrestricted and very largely unfished resource. The emphasis will be on fly and, no doubt, catch and release – all very laudable in its own way but not necessarily for me. In the end, as with most of my fishing today, I am happy to make do with the glad memories born of the opportunities that were afforded me in my youth.

The Lure of Salmon

For years, the pursuit of salmon was of no interest to me. Something about my upbringing and development as a fisherman made the catching of salmon something of an irrelevance. Salmon fishing seemed at best to be the far-off and inaccessible pursuit of the select few – mostly, the few with money to spend. It took years for this delusion to be dispelled but, at the time, it was an unquestioned assumption that resulted in any talk of salmon being dismissed outright, to be replaced by thoughts of more accessible quarry such as trout and grayling. I bore no grudge towards those who fished for salmon. I had, after all, access to a myriad of excellent trout waters, not least in the Scottish Borders and far-flung Sutherland that would take a lifetime and more to explore. Why bother with salmon when so overwhelmingly hooked on the pursuit of trout? Why indeed! And yet, something happened over a period of years that resulted in salmon fishing becoming an obsession and the pursuit of trout becoming something of much less importance, something to be tasted and savoured on a very few occasions each season. Today, I spend hours and days in pursuit of salmon as if there was no tomorrow. There may be something profoundly appropriate in this assertion – who knows how long the pursuit of Atlantic salmon by sport fishermen will remain a viable option? How I envy those of a previous generation for whom the conservation of precious stock was not a matter of concern. Fishing huts with their pictures and logbooks are littered with the documentation of phenomenal – at least in the context of current times – catches. How things have changed! And the perverse corollary to all of this is that fishing rods, lines and, indeed, flies have all developed into weaponry whose efficiency far exceeds that wielded by our predecessors. What would those of a previous generation have given to cast with our light and balanced rods as opposed to the heavy wands of their time? They caught fish because there were fish to catch – a scenario that most definitely is not always the case today! Salmon fishing is not generally difficult but, to be consistently successful, there must be fish in the river and you must be in the right place at the right time, all assuming a measure of competence in placing a line on the water. Previously, on association water, catching of salmon was relatively easy to achieve by watching river levels and pouncing when the stars were aligned! I recently returned from a sortie on my local beat. The water was perfect, yet I caught nothing. I doubt if there were more than one or two fish – if any – in the whole beat. Worse still was the information – so readily available today – that, of the beats that report catches, only one fish had been caught on the river all week and this in the previously prime second week of May. What a disaster! Fanatical as I may now be about my salmon fishing, I feel as though I am plying my art in the very death throw of a worthy tradition. The future looks grim but, you never know, things may improve. I do hope so.

So, what got me started; why the shift in focus? Strangely – given our Scottish salmon tradition – the initial spark came from acquaintances in Sweden who were becoming increasingly interested in the pursuit of both trout and salmon. Our early focus was on catching salmon and sea trout in Älvkarleby – a rapidly flowing hydro water, somewhat reminiscent of the lower Tay. To this end, I bought, through a mail order firm in the north of England, a fifteen-foot Daiwa CF98 rod, a Daiwa reel, a sinking line (that later proved to be a good catcher of fish) and a floating line that immediately proved to be an abomination! Add to this, some heavy-duty nylon and an uninspiring selection of heavy tube flies, a pair of Ocean chest waders (good buy at the time) and a Hardy wading jacket (which, although too small, is still going strong) and you have an almost-complete picture of me the intrepid, would-be salmon fisher! Of course, it was all enthusiasm with any smidgen of competence being at a real premium. I had seen pictures of how to Spey cast – how dreadful these diagrams can be – and, by painful trial and error, managed to propel assorted tube flies into battle. It was all tremendously hard work and quite uninformed but, as with all my fishing efforts, I had to start somewhere. What I would have given for a skilled mentor in those early days! I did catch sea trout but not many and none of them was of the calibre for which this river was noted. My friends and I did not catch salmon on our few attempts on this water but we did see fish being caught. My clearest memories are of one character up to his waist in fast flowing water, double-Spey casting a line square to the current and repeatedly hooking and, in one hectic period, repeatedly losing fish as a run of salmon went by his rod. It was all very reminiscent of what I have much more recently observed at Stormont on the river Tay. (The Stormont rods, however, seem to have a happy knack of landing a better quota of hooked fish than did my Älvkarleby fisher!) I also have very vivid memories of one 'worthy', cycling home along the banks of Älvkarleby, with his morning catch draped from the handle bar, a glistening fish in the 20-lb category. What a sight; what a memory! I can still see the smile of contentment on his face.

It does seem fitting that it should have been back in Scotland – the home of much to do with the traditions of fly-fishing – where I was to catch my first salmon. I had read about the river Moriston and its unusual Estuary beat in a fine and informative publication written by Bill 'Rogie' Brown about salmon fishing in Scotland. Rogie provided useful and, in the case of the Moriston, mouth-watering gems of information about different Scottish beats and, crucially, how and when to access them. The problem with all such sources of information is that they soon become dated and to all intents and purposes irrelevant to current situations. However, at the time, Rogie's book on salmon beats ranked in my estimation alongside Bruce Sandison's book on the trout lochs of Scotland. Both books provided invaluable information on Scottish fishing and its availability. When it came to the river Moriston, Rogie pulled no punches. On its day, the Moriston could be quite magnificent. Where else could boast a day with five fish in the 30-lb category? Where indeed! But then – as in so much else – there is a down side. The Moriston flows into the north shore of loch Ness and its Estuary beat is very short. It is also subject to extremes of flow, being part of a hydro scheme. When the generators are on, the river flows majestically with a lively and enticing push of water throughout the entire length of the beat, in all not more than a few hundred metres. Spring is the time to be there and, when the water is on, this beat provides a fantastic opportunity of catching a prime springer. There is no more lovely fish to be caught and not a lovelier place to catch it. However, if the water is off, the flow diminishes to a trickle as both water and fish leave the beat. There is even a rebound effect where water from the loch pushes back into the estuary and, for a few minutes, the flow of the river is reversed! In visiting the Moriston, you pray for a cold snap down south so that the generators will be doing their stuff and the river and its fish are in fine ply. It is all a bit unreliable – hence its very reasonable price tag – but, on its day, it is a true gem of a beat.

My first acquaintance with the Moriston was a fleeting summer trip at the completely wrong time of year – a mistake not to be repeated. When I did eventually arrive at the right time, the snow was still on the adjacent hilltops and the early April weather was keen. Crucially, the generators were on and I had a rod for a couple of days, with the chance of an evening cast on arrival. This was when I first met Alistair who was the Moriston ghillie at that time. He used to be a ghillie on the Brora, a river of whose praises he sang highly, but he had moved to the Glenmoriston Estate some years prior to my first visit. Our first acquaintance was when, on arrival, I found Alistair felling trees on the far bank opposite the fishing hut, with logs and branches crashing into the deep water! Most of these logs were retrieved by Alistair but, to my way of thinking, the whole activity did not bode particularly well for an early evening cast. Alistair knew differently and convinced me to waste no further time but to get stuck in with good prospects of a fish, many of which he assured me were in the beat. Good ghillies are always optimistic! I can recall the occasion clearly. The water was cold and Ocean waders were never renowned for their warmth! I was up to my waist midstream, wading down from the hut and fishing towards the far bank where Alistair's tree felling had now stopped for the day. It was a glorious evening but the cold was making me shiver and my hands were numb. The sinking line was going out pretty well, not spectacularly long casts but sufficient to let the fly swing at depth some twenty yards below me. It was a case of a couple of steps forward, a few pulls on the line and a roll cast to get the fly up, then an overhead cast to get the fly angled towards the far bank; perhaps a rapid mend to slow the fly before the line sank. Then there was the wait, feeling for the pull of line and fly as they swung below me, before repeating the whole process. I was slowing things down, very slow now just as Bill Currie had advocated in his writing, getting down where the fish were and showing them something they would not have to chase far in the cold water. I sensed the Black and Yellow tube patrolling the depths as I waded easily and slowly downstream over the gravel bed. I did not know what to expect but I had sufficient confidence in the way things were going to assume that I was on the right track. The line was straightening and the brass tube was sinking and moving slowly. This all seemed to tie in with what I had read about spring fishing in cold water. I had touched the gravel bottom a couple of times, not real snags but enough to know that the fly was fishing at depth. The actual take, when it came, was a solid pull on the line that was quite different from any previous knocks and bumps. When I bent into the fish, I had the thrill of feeling its pulsating weight before it moved steadily down and towards the far bank. This was different from anything I had experienced previously. The fight was solid and the runs were strong without being particularly spectacular or hectic. I have since found this to be the case with lots of Moriston fish. These early arrivals have travelled rapidly up Loch Ness and must enter the Moriston following considerable exertion. In the cold, spring water, you feel their weight and strong pulls but they do not exhibit the manic runs and splashing of their much smaller relatives, the strong grilse of warmer summer waters. Spring fish are, however, arguably the supreme trophy in salmon fishing. They are often amongst the largest fish of the season and their appearance is without equal. When I eventually beached my prize, its strong silver flanks reflected the last of the evening light. It had that stunning but subtle touch of magenta that I have only seen on fresh-run springers and is completely different from the silver of summer salmon and grilse and any redness seen in the shine of later-season fish. My fish was not particularly large, weighing only nine pounds. But it was my first salmon. Indeed, it was the first salmon I had hooked, so I was fortunate not to have gone through the agony of losing such a trophy when it first came my way. However, the dull disappointment of fish lost was very soon to be experienced when, on the following day, I fought and lost a much larger fish in the same stream. I saw this fish and it remains one of the biggest fish I have ever hooked. To this day, I have kept the small treble that was sadly-mangled and destroyed by this leviathan. Such is the lot of the ardent salmon fisher: One day the ecstasy of success, the next day the agony of failure. Salmon fishing is not only obsessive; it can traverse the whole range of emotions from joy to downright frustration and despondency. Of course, the true addict always returns for more, be it joy or pain!

I have fished the Moriston on many subsequent occasions, although not so frequently in more recent years. It is intriguing water and can yield large fish. Twenty pounds was a good fish for my friends and myself although I know of larger fish in the years I fished, alas not the thirty-pounders of bygone years. Like most salmon fisheries, its past was probably more impressive than its present but it remains a top prospect for an early fish. I once managed a springer on the first Saturday of the season in mid-January, a lovely fish of thirteen pounds, fresh from the sea. I know of rods who have managed three or four fish in a day but that is exceptional. It requires an element of skill but also a large measure of luck. If you are fishing when the run comes in, then you stand a very good chance of connecting. The fish seem to arrive in pods of a few fish, not many but perhaps three or four fish at a time. It is not all luck, of course. I remember one occasion when I was one of three rods who had fished all day without success. Alastair arrived on the water in the later afternoon to enquire of our day and seemed surprised that we had not had more success. On learning that we had seen a few fish, he promptly moved upstream on the beat and within a few casts had connected with and landed a real beauty of fourteen pounds. He knew exactly what he was doing and it was good to see him in action. It was perhaps less exciting and verging on embarrassing when the same scenario was repeated the following evening! He had exuded confidence and expected to catch fish on both occasions, although he later divulged that even he was surprised about the repeat performance! We were left with mixed feelings of admiration and inadequacy but fortunately were also encouraged to continue our efforts. We did eventually get into fish! Alastair's approach was interesting. By early April, he had mainly abandoned any thought of sinking lines and big flies. His standard spring gear was a fifteen-footer, although I have seen him on the Moriston with an eighteen-foot rod and a sink-tip line. His fly was invariable something that he called a 'Tosh' although it bore no resemblance to bought dressings of that name. His fly dressings were minimal, comprising a half-inch tube made from black cable sleeving on to which a ring of yellowish-brown squirrel hair was tied at the head. That was it. The whole fly was less than an inch in length and looked distinctly scrubby, the sort of thing that would never be displayed in a shop because nobody would buy it! A treble was threaded into the tube and action would commence. His standard practice was to cast the most exquisite of overhead lines, placing twenty-five to thirty yards of line on the water, the fly kicking out ahead of the line. He would then tuck his rod under his arm and start hand-lining the contraption for several yards as it slowly swung in the current. The takes were solid and the rod would be raised. It was a joy to listen to the ensuing fight as every twist and turn of the fish was countered with rye comment from its captor. He always talked of the likelihood of losing a fish, depending on how it had been hooked and which way it had turned as it took the fly. I never saw him lose one.

There were days when the fishing was outstanding. I recall one occasion when I had arranged to meet Carlo on the water. The plan was to get started on arrival. I arrived shortly before nine in the morning. By this time, Carlo had two fish on the bank and had lost a third. I soon got one and lost another. If I recall correctly, Carlo got one more before all went quiet – and it was only ten o'clock in the morning. They were all cracking fish and seemed to be particularly keen on grabbing a yellowish shrimp pattern with a hair wing sporting greenish additions, all dressed on a large silver-grey double. In these days, you would be hard pressed to find better spring fishing in Scotland. I know Carlo returned for several years but he never had quite the same experience again. It must rate as one of his most memorable days and it was a joy to be part of it.

There are many other happy memories from the Moriston. One was notable because of its unexpected moment. It involved Dennis – a ghillie on the Tay of whom I write elsewhere. Dennis was never one to be flustered. He combined a fine and canny fishing knowledge with an indomitable spirit and wit, attributes that must have been crucial to his profession. One of the marks of a good ghillie is his ability to encourage further endeavour when things are depressingly slow on the river. Rods will all vary in competence but even the best can lose heart when not much is happening. This does not matter on home waters to which one has easy and ready access because the sensible option can be to pack up and return another day. But this is not a viable option where an invitation has been given or money has been spent on a relatively exclusive beat. The onus is on the rods to fish even when the going is tough. It is precisely then that the unbounded optimism and encouragement of a man such as Dennis is invaluable. Dennis always enjoyed the 'social' and was at the heart of all good banter in his Tay hut before dispatching his rods, always with the sage advice: "Remember, there's no limit!" Whatever, he was never short of a story. At the Moriston, he was the epitome of combined composure and narrative, as he expounded on some obscure story – if I recall correctly relating to Raigmore Hospital. He was casting nonchalantly across the pool above the hut as he addressed the assembled rods and ghillie, right hand lightly holding the rod as the fly swung in the slowish water, left hand gesticulating as he emphasised the points he was making. When the fish took, I swear he neither batted an eyelid nor missed a stroke in his story telling and hand waving. It was the ultimate demonstration of how to let a salmon hook itself. His narration continued with full composure as he played the fish to the net. Dennis never said much about the incident but I have a suspicion that he took enormous pleasure in hooking and landing this fish without the least perturbation to his train of thought and demeanour – the epitome of fishing ease and so typical of the man.

Rogie provoked another series of sorties, this time to the River Nith in south-west Scotland. These were autumnal visits made in the company of Swedish friends to the Midnithsdale stretch at Thornhill. This was always busy fishing with locals and visitors alike lining the banks. We did get fish – not many and none of them spectacularly large – but the experience helped hone what limited skills I had acquired elsewhere. The increasingly short autumn days with all their subtle harbingers of death and decay were in stark contrast to the keen and lively awakening of spring fishing in the Highlands. The sharp edge to colours and sound that heralded the onset of spring was replaced by the diffuse washed-out hues of late summer, splashed with the raw redness and gold of encroaching autumn. These visuals of seasonal change were reflected in the choice of fly patterns where red and orange predominated in contrast to the yellow and black of spring. Here, you could fish with fly or worm and, when the water was high, by spinner. To begin with, I fished fly, because that is what I had done previously when trout fishing and because that is how I had started my salmon fishing. However, my times on the Nith overlapped with the start of my times on the Tay where I was rapidly getting into the way of worm fishing and how effective that could be. So, although I caught some Nith fish on the fly, I caught as many and more on the worm. The last day I fished Midnithsdale, I had the satisfaction of landing two salmon, both on the worm. One was taken from a favourite pool and the other from a relatively unfished bank near the top of the beat. The latter fish was slightly coloured as were many of the fish at this time of year but the other was a stunningly beautiful fish, fresh to the river. By this time, I knew what I was doing with the worm, at least sufficiently so to expect success. On that day, I felt I could have caught more but, strangely, I had no appetite to continue. Two fish on the worm when others were not catching much seemed sufficient. Most rods would fish the worm on this stretch and, with some notable exceptions, seemed to fare better than those who fished fly. The worm was, of course, fished with varying degrees of competence but I have a suspicion that it was mainly fished in a manner that was less detrimental to the efforts of others than was much of the fly fishing. If worm fishing was associated with mixed competence on this busy water, then fly fishing was practised with an even wider range of expertise. At that time, I most definitely belonged to the ranks of those whose enthusiasm for fly fishing far outstripped their ability. Heavy fly lines would incessantly thrash and splash the lies where fish showed and this can only have been detrimental to the chance of success for one and all. There were exceptions. I recall speaking to a fisher whose double-Spey cast was effortless and accurate – a delight to watch. He was a Spey ghillie whose season had by this time closed. He was in the habit of visiting Midnithsdale for a late-season cast and did not seem too perturbed by the mixed ability of other rods. I suppose he would have experienced the full range of ability on his own beat. I am not critical of those who splash and crash about the water; after all, we must all get started somewhere. However, repeated and incessant disturbance is a bit of a deterrent to serious investment in fishing time and, where opportunities arise elsewhere, is likely to result in fewer visits by those who have honed their skills. For whatever reason, my day with two fish on the worm has been my last on this lovely stretch of water. These sorties were my introduction to late autumn fishing and I cherish the memory. I can still sense the encroaching mist as the light fades from a red sunset and the weary, contented trudge back to the village, infused by the tang of smoke from coal fires, shortly to provide warmth as the coldness of another autumn night takes grip. It is time, with glass in hand, to pull a chair to the fire and share the camaraderie of those for whom the river is everything – a camaraderie that spawns enthusiasm for renewed efforts the following day. Wonderful!

Reflections on my early efforts at luring salmon would be incomplete without mention of the Tweed, one of the big four in the Scottish heritage. My experience of the Tweed was – and remains – very limited. I was fortunate to be invited for a cast on the upper river during the autumn months. My first experience of the beat was amongst my best, all of which have been determined by prevailing water conditions. I recall the torrential rain and flood on the Sunday preceding my Monday visit. I also recall being amazed at how quickly the river cleared and the level dropped as I fished. The fishing was not spectacular but I did hook and land a fine eleven-pound fish on a sinking line and a dark Willie Gunn variant. The occasion is memorable partly because of the difficulty I experienced in landing the fish. This fish had no interest in coming ashore and seemed intent on hugging the depths of the fast stream in which it was hooked. I went above it to no avail and then applied pressure from below its lie – same result! When I eased the strain, my fish went on tour and, after some determined rushes, it came eventually into the quieter water near my bank. I landed the fish but I never felt in control throughout proceedings and I concluded that I might benefit from a rod with a bit more 'backbone'. Daiwa have made some great rods over the years – my Alltmor eleven-footer is a real gem – but the CF98 which had served me so well now seemed to lack a bit of power when it came to playing heavier fish in fast water. Soon afterwards, I invested in a Bruce and Walker Powerlite fifteen-footer. When required, its reserves of power have never let me down, either when casting or playing a heavy fish. Twenty years on, it continues to be my weapon of choice for much of my fishing when there is a good push of water. For me, its lighter cousin – the Bruce and Walker Norway – takes over when water conditions are a bit less demanding of the sheer power that comes with the Powerlite. The Norway is lighter than the Powerlite although, with a proper balance of line, rod and reel, I have never found weight to be a decisive factor. In the end, it is all a matter of preference – the touch and feel of the assembled gear – that determines my choice between these two superb rods. For those with an appreciation of such things, it will be apparent that my preference has been for traditional (long head-length) Spey casting. This goes against the current trend of using shorter head lengths but it is what I enjoy and, until I am convinced of any downright inadequacy of my approach – and this may very well be forthcoming – it is what I shall continue to use. In the past couple of seasons, I have got into the way of using Guideline triple-density heads (things are getting awfully complicated!) and I have found these to be wonderful casters on my Bruce and Walker rods (for which they were never intended). However, there remains an intrinsic beauty in watching a devotee of full-Spey lines slowly but easily unfurl a cast of thirty-plus yards towards the far bank – always with a small kick of the fly as more line is pulled from the reel. Poetry in motion indeed!

These early sorties – Moriston, Nith and Tweed – laid the foundations for what was to follow on the Tay and, ultimately, elsewhere. We all continue to learn throughout our fishing lives but most of us can possibly identify stages, times of small achievement, that conferred a measure of confidence and encouraged us to continue and to improve. It is surely a sorry day when a fisherman feels he has no more to learn. We may all become relatively expert on certain waters but it only requires a new challenge – an invitation to fish water with which we are unfamiliar – for the limitations to our experience and competence to be rudely exposed. The mark of progress towards competence in our fishing is surely the ease with which we adapt to a new circumstance. Having got started and having acquired a measure of rudimentary proficiency in my salmon fishing, my challenge – the opportunity to learn and progress – was to be the river Tay. As challenges go, it was not trivial. To this day, it provides me with a fascinating wealth of opportunity to hone my skills in the company of those who know and fish this river with so much more proficiency than I can ever dare dream of attaining. They are the fishers who maintain and develop our traditions; they are the fishers from whom it has been my privilege to learn.

Feeling for the Tay

In the Scottish context, the Tay is a big river. In all its length – and in this I include its many tributaries – it is both wild and serene. It is also distinctly dangerous in its seductive beauty. Its banks are not for the faint-hearted. A careless approach, a stumble here, a fall there or a slither in the shingle and you can be heading to the hut for a change of clothes or much worse. When I fished its banks, I knew it to host three deaths: Two untimely and tragic drownings and one departure – equally tragic – of one for whom death seemed the better option. And all of this on the one beat that came to mean so much to me. I know of further mishaps on other beats.

The Tay is a river that means so many different things to the many who fish its length. To some, it is all about the challenge and occasional success of catching the fish of a lifetime. It is a river system where the chances of doing so are much greater than in many of its Scottish neighbours. For many, it has superb reaches for the pursuit of the much sought-after springer. On the beat I fished most, I have opened its account in the cold of March but never earlier. For some, the Tay is the place of regular companionship or perhaps occasional solitude in the relaxed pursuit of summer fish, irrespective of their size. I have experienced wonderful July evenings when the grilse have decided to 'play' just as the heat of the day recedes and darkness encroaches – a truly magic time. A couple of weeks' later and my evening rod has been well and truly bent to the surging runs of heavy August fish. These are harbingers of the autumn run, a prolific push of fish that for many rods epitomises – or at least, it used to – the essence of Tay fishing. I have tasted it all; I have loved it all. It is unlikely that this majestic river means the same to any two people. For all who walk its banks or wade its shingle beds, it is a complex mosaic of streams and pools with myriad features, all fascinating in different ways and always changing as the weather and light shift with day and season. It is big and mostly incomprehensible in its movement. For Bill Currie, this is the river that should be considered as having rivers within rivers. In appreciating this, perhaps only then can you get to grips with its true potential as a fishery. You cannot fish it all so, when the opportunity arises, concentrate on the stream that is accessible, the one that is within reach. Tomorrow is another day and the rivers within rivers will have changed.

The Kercock beat – the one I fished most – is a middle beat, one of those whose vast white shingle beds are mostly flanked by open grassy banks interspersed with occasional wooded stretches. It is mostly double-bank fishing and this can be a great advantage in that the water you fish at the start of a day has not been disturbed; fish may have settled in the first light and may be catchable. It is not the most renowned beat nor is it the most prolific but it has some superb runs and pools. For those with eyes to see and ears to hear, it is a place of wonder. I have walked its banks at all seasons but no occasion is more glorious than the late spring and early summer. Then you can marvel at its abundance of nesting birds – plovers and sandpipers, oystercatchers and gulls, finches, tits and thrushes. It is the feeding ground of ospreys and the nesting site of visiting martins and kingfisher. Otters and stoats abound; sit still and quietly and you will see them all. Its banks are covered in the most wonderful display of flowering herbs and grasses, early displays of cowslip and campion with later abundance of forget-me-not, harebells, ragwort, lupin, willow herbs and meadow sweet, all complemented by the heady scent of marjoram, sage and thyme and much more.

I fished Kercock over a period of some twenty years and have some wonderful memories of its richness. Yet, in a strangely indefinable way, it remains a mystery. After all these years, I feel that I have only scratched the surface of its wealth. This river keeps flowing from day to day and season to season, sculpting depths and shallows as it goes. It is never static. If on occasion it was generous in its return, any assumption of real acquaintance and knowledge was soon dismissed as the one scenario of depths and shallows was replaced by another and the very mood of the place changed. I have not fished this beat in recent years and now have no real enthusiasm to do so. I hope it may delight those who still fish its banks but I fear it might disappointment me. It was central to my development as a salmon fisher but it was much more than that. It was a place where I found friendship and learnt a great deal about myself and many others who made it their home. And all this happened through Dennis, the man who pulled the strings, the man who was the very heart beat of the place. When this man's tenure as ghillie terminated, then my enthusiasm for the place died.

The pattern of its rod fishing changed and not to my liking. I hope a new cohort of fishers has found a home on this beat and I hope their experience is good. However, it will be very different from mine.

When Dennis started, he lay down the rules. His interview for the position of ghillie involved a panel comprising the then Lord Perth and his estate factor. The story goes that when intimated by the factor that part of the ghillie's remit was to maintain the grassy banks and that a scythe would be provided to that end, Dennis was not slow in his retort: If and only if an axe was provided for the estate forester, then he – Dennis – would contemplate the use of a scythe. Apparently, Lord Perth was greatly amused; what the factor thought is less clear! Whatever, the banks were subsequently maintained by means other than a scythe. The outcome of this early assertion of rights and expectations was a burgeoning mutual respect between His Lordship and his newly appointed ghillie, a respect that deepened through the years. Dennis always had the trust of his employer to do what was right for the beat and the rods who fished its banks. In return, Dennis met the very few demands of his employer – normally, the very occasional expectation of His Lordship having sole access to the beat and that his guests enjoyed their days on the beat. This did not seem to amount to more than a very few days each season, which meant that to all intents and purposes, the beat was run by Dennis and this he did in a scrupulously fair and generous manner.

It so happens that I started fishing Kercock when Dennis started as ghillie. At the time, most of the fishing was let on a weekly basis to parties of four of five rods. You paid your way and you and your party had sole access. For most of the week, you fished the lower beat; on alternate years, you had either one or two days on the upper beat. This arrangement reflected the beat ownership at the time, His Lordship having full riparian rights on the lower beat and shared rights on the upper. In practice, the arrangement meant that our party of rods had effective double-bank fishing throughout. What a joy! The rules were gloriously simple. Dennis expected mutual respect amongst rods and between rods and himself. If you followed this easy code of conduct, then you were a welcome guest. No one would lay claim to the best water to the exclusion of others; rods rotated in a carefree and easy manner that let everyone fish with high expectation. No one fished in a manner that was to the detriment of others; everyone got their chance. All in all, it was very uncomplicated and led to a relaxed and easy friendship amongst rods. For the few who did not meet this basic expectation of civility, they encountered the other face of Dennis the manager. In short, they were not welcome and did not return. Simple but fair: If you met the basic expectation, you had the most wonderful and on-going experience. If you transgressed, then it was made clear that you would not be returning.

The weekly let with its daytime fishing was the very backbone of all that followed. From the outset, the offer of evening fishing was made at the discretion of Dennis. He quickly appraised his rods and, on the assumption of fair play when he was not in attendance, those whom he trusted had the wonderful opportunity of evening and early morning casts. This was a fantastic opportunity and privilege that I cherished increasingly as the years went by. The offer was not of course extended exclusively to me but for many seasons, I was in effect the only member of our party who grasped the occasion. So, as the years went by, I would start by putting in a daytime shift often in low-water conditions and the fierce heat of an August sun. However, my heart was not always in the matter and my daytime efforts could be a bit sporadic, all because I knew that my best chance would come later as the sun first left the water and the evening cool encroached. And what a wonderful opportunity it was! I knew at the time that I was privileged in having such secluded access to the water; I appreciate it even more now that the opportunity has passed. Imagine having sole evening access to such stretches as the Cottage Stream and Dowie Burn; incredible but true – and not just once but on any occasion during my week! No wonder fish were caught! I never knew what might come next, perhaps a couple of lively grilse to the worm at the drop-off in the Cottage Stream or perhaps a heavier fish to the fly from the same stream as it started to swim from the far rapid depths below the gate and birch tree to the quieter shallows on my bank. There was always the high expectation of success and often it was fulfilled. As the evening progressed, the once chattering river would assume an increasingly serene and mysterious mood. The last light would fade in pastel or sometimes starker shades and the boundaries between trees, grass, shingle and water would merge into a shady whole. The takes would no longer be so forthcoming and it would be time to turn my back on the water and walk wearily towards the hut, tired but elated and often with fish in hand. A cup of coffee from the kettle under the light of the fuel lamp would suffice to keep me awake before the drive home. Then a few hours' sleep would be grasped before an early start the following morning. What fishing! What memories and what a privilege!

The next 'concession' was the invitation to fish this beat at times other than during my regular week. What a joy it was to come home from work or to be summoned from the garden to learn that Dennis was on the phone asking if I wanted to come 'out to play'! The rapid throwing of tackle into the car and the carefree rush to Kercock became a frequent occurrence. And then came the most incredibly generous of invitations: The encouragement from Dennis that I should make the call anytime to enquire if I might come down for a cast. What utter generosity on his part! There were other rods who shared this privilege and we all owe so much to Dennis for the opportunity he afforded us. No doubt, our fitful efforts contributed to the season's tally for the beat but the open invitation was based on much more than any desire to keep the tally moving. It was an expression of friendship on the river, a friendship based on a shared enthusiasm for the water and its fish and for the glorious place through which it flowed. It was a friendship based on the enjoyment of others. Our presence and companionship were in some unspoken way based on a shared custody of a once great resource and tradition. Our common enthusiasm for access to this magic place and its welfare for which Dennis strived was what mattered and not the mere number or size of fish caught, although the latter were of course part of the rich tapestry.

So, what of fish caught? There were a few! Strangely, Kercock was not a beat where I recall losing many fish. Perhaps this is because, especially during my early years, I fished the worm a great deal. The advice, assuming you wished to keep a fish, was that you could not be too slow in striking or tightening once you had felt a fish knocking on the worm. This 'knocking' is at the heart of worm fishing. It is one of the most enthralling of fishing experiences, the very essence of the pursuit! You must imagine the cast – slightly upstream – then the feel for the lead weight (yes, we fished lead in those days) as it starts to trundle across the far shingle and boulders. Not too fast or it will be mostly fruitless, nor too slow or you would snag or catch eels; always the adjustment of lead weighting, the extent of upstream angle in the cast and the amount of line released before making and keeping contact as lead and worm progressed downstream. The trundling lead is felt as an incessant – sometimes intermittent – tapping on the river bed. If you watch the rod tip, you will see it shivering and you may release a little more line. A step downstream as you wind in the bait and then the whole thing can be repeated. You soon learn where the taking spots are in a pool and expectation heightens as one of these is approached. You can shut your eyes and fish the worm! In fact, one of its main proponents at Kercock was Tommy and he was profoundly blind. If the first spot does not produce the goods, then you assume that the fish have fallen back slightly in the pool; you just know they are there! And then comes the knock. It is completely different from the trundling that you have been feeling throughout the approach. It is a cross between a pull and a pulse, something distinctly different from the previous tapping. You do not strike. It can be wise to release a yard or two of line; some rods prefer to do nothing. You may feel the attack a second time. Perhaps pay out a further couple of yards. Nothing happens. Slowly – very slowly – you wind in some line and feel for the fish. Another determined knock! The choice is yours. I would generally tighten hard into the fish at this point, others would give it another couple of knocks before doing so. Whatever, once hooked, a salmon on the worm generally means a salmon on the bank. It is all very tactile and all very exciting!

I did catch quite a few fish on the worm. My two best fish were summer salmon of sixteen pounds – real beauties both! On one memorable occasion, I arrived at the tail of the Garden pool on the upper beat just after the other rods had finished in the early evening. The sunlight was still strong but different from that of the afternoon. There was now a diffuse golden-yellow gleam to the light as the sun lowered on the horizon and the shadows lengthened. I recall the fish taking in fast water in a bulge above a massive concrete block that had made an appearance midstream in the tail of the Garden pool that season. I have no idea on the origins of this feature. It lacked any aesthetic attributes but, while it was there, the salmon loved it! I was fishing a heavy weight for the light rod – Dennis referred to it in unfavourable terms as my 'woman's rod'. Whatever, it caught me many fish and was very sensitive to the taps and knocks of the worm. I eventually had this fish tired and ready for the beach but landing it was tricky. The only viable option was to ease the fish into a small pocket of quieter water fringed by willow sprouts at the very tail of the Garden before it rushed into the neck of the Dungeon below. Tricky stuff indeed! I managed to steer the fish on to the shelving bank – almost – on five occasions before finally getting hold of the wrist on its tail and heaving it unceremoniously ashore. It was this experience and one other with a lively eleven-pounder at the Green Bank that convinced me that a rod with more spine might be advantageous. Through Dennis, I was soon the proud owner of a Bruce & Walker worming rod, a real beast of a rod! For all its strength, it had a wonderfully delicate touch and sensitivity. Snags on the riverbed became the exception rather than the rule; it now seemed possible to ease and edge the worm around boulders and other obstructions on its way downstream!

The second of my biggest fish to the worm was taken several years – and many fine Kercock salmon – later. I was fishing one summer evening and started at the inside neck of Dowie Burn. This pool is named after the often-choked stream that enters the main pool on its left-hand bank. It is not much more than a glorified ditch but it was the haunt of kingfishers and I suspect, when an autumn flood would clear any debris, it became the home of spawning salmon. Dowie was an intriguing pool to worm fish, not least because of the very real danger it posed to life and limb. It had a very fast and channelled neck that, when in flood, sculpted deep into its bed. Masses of white shingle formed an extensive apron of normally shallow water on the right-hand bank. In certain heights, the whole pool was one large eddy with the upstream flow on the edge between shingle apron and sudden depth. The danger lay in the steepness of its shingle banks. An unwary tread on the shelving shingle and you would be on a rolling treadmill that defied your desperate attempts to back out of the pool. I have encountered this elsewhere on the Tay and it is not a happy experience. I have been fortunate to walk away from this type of hazard; others have been less fortunate. The two accidental drownings at Kercock to which I have referred were both associated with Dowie, one directly so where the body was retrieved from the pool, the other of less certain cause where the body was recovered a short distance downstream at the foot of the beat. These tragic instances are salutary reminders that fishing is not entirely without danger. On the day in question, I had just made a cast or two and had decided that a change in lead weight was in order. I had reeled in my bait and was in the process of attaching a heavier lead when an otter showed close to the edge of the far bank. Sighting of otters at Kercock was far from unusual and careful observation could identify the likely location of a holt. However, in this instance, the otter was not alone. A great deal of splashing revealed the presence of two otters at play. They promptly left the stream and continued their play on a small sandy spit immediately downstream of the burn mouth. This spit was no more than a few yards in length and was tight against steep banking. The pair seemed quite oblivious to my presence some twenty yards distant; either that or they considered me harmless and therefore of no consequence to their fun. Whatever, the amazing spectacle continued for several minutes. It was quite enthralling and, unlike most theatre, appeared to have no scheduled breaks between acts! Although the evening was not late and despite the marvellous spectacle afforded by the cavorting couple, I felt – as ever – that fishing time was precious. What if I was to try a tentative cast; would the show go on or would the curtain come down? I was intrigued that the otters did not seem to mind my presence. Would a cast disturb them? There is no way that a one-and-a-half-ounce lead weight can enter the water on the back of a twenty-yard cast without making a splash! The dilemma was that to make the cast worthwhile, the lead would have to enter the water close to the sandy spit – in my experience one of the best taking spots. Nothing venture, nothing gained! Out went the lead and bait with the resultant splash on entry, the whole assembly landing some two or three yards upstream of the spit with its otters. Did they react to the splash? Not in any way that I noticed and they surely could not have missed the intrusive entry. Whatever, they seemed gloriously unconcerned by the event. The worm trundled past the expected taking spot at the sandy spit without interruption but there were other spots to be explored as I slowly worked the worm back to my stance in readiness for the next cast. I mentioned that Dowie was deep, what with its shelving shingle banks. Its depths certainly exceeded five metres in some parts and I suspect that it had pots and channels whose depths were well in excess of that figure. Because of the eddy effect in this pool, it was always necessary to feel for the lead weight and pay or retrieve line as necessary. Careful management of the worm in this manner often resulted in solid pulls being felt as it explored the steep sloping shingle banks. I knew there was the possibility of a take but surely, it would not happen at this of all moments. But, of course, it did! The knock was unmistakeable, the resolute pulling of a fish at the worm. Once, twice, three times, then the firm bending of the rod into the weight of the fish – and this one was heavy! I guess you can only smile when this sort of thing happens. Here I was, attached to a hefty salmon near two otters at play. There were many possible outcomes but, from the outset, the fish dictated matters. As soon as it was hooked, it made a determined rush to the far bank, apparently intent on joining the otters on the spit. As it hit the shallows, it rocketed out of the water and came clattering down with one almighty splash. Even the otters thought better of hanging around and they were in the stream in a flash, the rainbow spray of their entry at one with that of the salmon. I have no idea whether the otters paid the fish any further attention but I suspect not. It was almost as if the fish had decided first things first: Let's get rid of any audience before getting down to business! The fight was hard and mostly deep but confined to the pool. When the fish tired, I eventually brought it to the surface up the face of the shingle bank very much in the style of pumping a large pollack from the base of a vertical sea cliff. That is an indication of how steep and deep are the banks of Dowie Burn. Of course, once the fish had surfaced, it was a relatively easy matter to walk it across the shallow apron and beach it on the shingle edge. What a beauty it was, glistening in the low evening sun!

There are so many more fine memories from worming on hot summer days and the encroaching darkness of Kercock evenings. Small pods of glistening grilse would be intercepted as they splashed through the beat. Dull days and slow times would suddenly be interrupted by hectic activity. I recall struggling one year when our week on the river was dreadfully slow. There just did not seem to be fish in the beat. They would of course be there but they just did not seem catchable – not by our party at any rate! I had slogged away for a week when my son Euan arrived unannounced on the beat. He had just arrived from Sweden some few hours previously on a visit to our family. He knew I would be fishing and, promptly, on being met at the airport by his mother, enquired if they could make a homeward diversion via Kercock. Now Catriona did not know her way to the beat, its exact location being one of my better-kept secrets but Euan did! So, the agreement was that, if he gave the directions, then Catriona would drop him off at the beat. On arrival, they caught Dennis just before his departure for the day and, in inimitable fashion, he made them immediately welcome and gladly provided Euan with all the necessary gear. No doubt, he told Euan to get stuck in, reminding him that there was no limit and, no doubt, also informing him of his father's complete lack of success. Euan greeted me as evening fell on the Cottage Stream, for my money the real 'jewel in the crown' of the beat. I was thrilled that he was there and that he should have had such enthusiasm for meeting me on the beat. However, I had real misgivings about his prospects in the remaining couple of hours that day. If it was not his first cast, it must have been his second and he was into a fish! I could not have been more thrilled; nor could Dennis when the story was recounted the following morning! Later, Dennis took great delight when submitting his catch report to the angling press in telling all and sundry of Euan's immediate success in the face of sustained and abject failure on the part of his father. He did, however, have the good grace to say something along the lines: "His father, who had been fishing all week without success, eventually caught…" What a concession and all so typical of the banter we shared on the riverbank! In writing this, I recall that Euan had out-fished me previously. For many seasons, he joined me for a day during my week at Kercock and, when I hooked a fish, I would pass him my rod. All good and well but of course the great thing would be to hook and land a fish himself. One evening, we were fishing the upper beat. Euan was on the right-hand bank at the tail of the Garden and I had crossed over to the left-hand bank, upstream of where he was fishing. We were both on the worm and neither of us had any success. As the light faded, I decided it was high time for me to cross the shallow rapids at the tail of Boatlands above the rush of water at the Garden neck. I shouted across to Euan that it was time to stop for the night and that I would join him at the head of the Garden on his side of the river. When I eventually got across the shallows, I was surprised that he was not there to meet me. This meant that, in waiting for him, we would have to stumble along the bank side in the dark. I could vaguely make out his silhouette at the foot of the Garden and he most certainly was not intent on making his way back up the beat. He was of course otherwise engaged having got stuck into a fish just after we had spoken! He took it all in his stride and assured me that, if only I would relax and be less anxious, he had the matter under control and would land his fish without any undue fuss. It proved to be a lovely fish of some eight-pounds weight and, most importantly, he had caught it all by himself despite my state of paternal panic. Walking back up the bank in total darkness was, of course, no problem at all.

Although I had several seasons at Kercock where I mostly fished worm, I reverted more and more to fly fishing. Dennis was a proponent of all methods. However, over the years he was increasingly encouraging many rods – if they were interested in doing so – to give the fly a proper shot. He made it his business to be proficient at casting – mostly Spey casting – and matters to do with tackle so that he could instruct his rods accordingly. When I got into fly fishing at Kercock, Dennis was a great proponent of Rio lines especially the Windcutter. These lines facilitated adequate casting with a modicum of expertise and many of us fished these lines at that time. Sometimes we fished them as full floaters; sometimes we attached leaders with different sink ratings. It was all a great and mutual learning experience. The same was true of rods. For years, the most popular of them all were the Bruce and Walker Norway series. When he retired from it all, Dennis passed on to me a Norway fifteen-footer. It is a great rod and I use it to this day. The same was of course also true of flies. Dennis was always open to ideas and would never be dogmatic. He would teach others and he would learn from others. His was a philosophy of sharing, always to the benefit of those that would listen. For Dennis, casting was always something that should be effortless. It was always salutary and a joy to behold when he made a cast to illustrate some point of improvement for one of his rods. He saw no need (in the main) to strive incessantly for the far bank in his casting. He was always surprised by the apparent insistence of so many rods to ignore the nearside water – especially at the start of a day – in their efforts to cover lies on the far side. He always believed that fish – not least spring fish – would be coming through the quieter and shallower water on the inside bend than in the main stream. Of course, his experience and advice related primarily to the Kercock beat. No doubt, there are occasions when the attainment of distance and or depth may be paramount to consistent success but, for many rods in many situations, adopting a quieter exploration of the nearer and shallower water with an easy style of casting might prove fruitful and enjoyable. Associated with any such strategy is the need for a careful approach to the stream. Dennis believed that it was to the detriment of their fishing and that of others that many rods announced their arrival at the stream by crunching their way across the shingle banks.

There were many marvellous times when fish fell to the fly but the most memorable are those associated with large fish and with greater numbers of fish. Early August at Kercock seemed to be a time when larger than average fish were often caught. The second week of August was one of high expectation. Fish from mid- to high-teens of pounds were the norm and fish in the low twenties were caught most seasons. Bigger fish were caught on the beat but these seemed to be occasional fish in the late-season run. I knew of some of these big August fish – I had even been on the water when they were caught but not present to witness their capture. The most memorable of those which I 'missed' was that of Carlo's twenty-two-pound fish from the Cottage stream, caught in the very last light of the evening. It was a truly magnificent fish and I was there for the photographs and celebrations in the hut! However, one night it was my turn to hook into one of these monsters. I was fishing down the Cottage stream with Billy and he was going first with a worm. I was following through with a very small Silver-Jungle-Stoat treble, a tiny fly with only wisps of dressing on a size-twelve gape. It was early evening, always a great time on the Cottage stream and the fish took as soon as the fly hit the far water at the gate above the birch. I bent into the fish and knew at once that it was exceptional. Not only was it big, it was indeed very heavy! It played hard which merited all the usual taunts and barbs from Billy about foul hooking and the like! But, this time, I knew differently and stuck to the matter of getting the leviathan ashore. Credit to Billy, he soon caught on to the idea of this fish being a bit out of the ordinary. When we did bring it in, it was massive. It was a cock fish with a massive head and the most savage look to its sunken eyes! It looked very different from any other 'big' fish I had landed. It was far from fresh but not too red; it had lost its silver flush and it must have been in the river for a few weeks. I decided that the fish would be returned and wished to do so without causing it any further distress. I wish I knew how big it was. Billy had no great enthusiasm for putting his hands anywhere near the mouth of this beast – and I do not blame him – but, fair play to him, without too much fuss and without removing the fish from the water, together we promptly freed the tiny treble from its jaws. I held the massive weight of the fish in the stream and can see it yet as it purposefully swam from my hands – an enormous olive-green shape disappearing into the depths of the stream. We did not quite know what to make of this fish. How big was it really? I do not know. There is, however, a sequel to the story that sheds some light on the matter. The very next evening Tommy was on the water accompanied by Billy. He had heard the story and was of course fishing a minute Silver-Jungle-Stoat. Tommy got his fish in the same stream as the previous night's capture and Billy was again there to give a hand. Tommy normally kept his fish and this one was no exception, although it was apparently less fresh than mine. Tommy's fish weighed twenty-two pounds. What interested me most was that Billy could confirm that the fish Tommy kept was most definitely not the same fish as I had caught and that my fish was much bigger! I have caught several fish around the twenty-pound mark – some under, some over – but this fish was so different from anything else I had caught. The eyes were strangely sunken in the skull and the girth was massive. I speculate on it being in the high twenties. In the end, all I can say is that it weighed more than twenty-two pounds.

The big-fish incident on the Cottage stream was important but there are other memorable occasions with the fly on the same stream. In my experience, the Cottage stream was the most productive fly water although I know Dennis highly rated the Croys on the lower beat. The occasion I remember most clearly is an evening when I took two fish and should have had three in a very short space of time. Now, you may think that this is nothing exceptional but, for the beat in question, it would generally have been pretty good-going. There are beats where you might expect to catch three or four times as many fish in short shrift but these are exceptions and they may be in very short supply in these currently lean times! As was often the case, I was fishing the Cottage stream on my own – company was great but solitude was a joy – and I just happened to intercept a run of fish. I was fishing the inside edge, having brought the fly across the fast stream off the lies on the far bank. I cannot be sure whether the fish followed my flies from the far bank across the stream or whether they intercepted the flies as they swam up the inside edge. In the end, it does not really matter. They took purposefully, with strong pulls to the fly in the near third of the river. As usual, these takes were opposite the gate and birch tree, a quite remarkable lie for taking fish. They were probably slightly further downstream than was often the case, indicating that the fish may very well have been coming up the inside edge, as opposed to having chased the fly from the far bank. They took solidly on a stripped-down Cascade double. The Cascade is a tremendously successful fly but often it is sold across the counter in unnecessarily heavy dressings. I am not sure why this should be the case; perhaps retailers wish to avoid customer complaints about not getting their money's worth! I tie most of my own flies but I often buy a Cascade dressing that I have found to be successful, providing I strip down its bulk. If it has silver tinsel strands in its wing, I remove all but one or two of them. I thin out the wing hairs by half; in like manner, the tail dressing. All in all, I end up with a very slim and unassuming fly that works well. Dennis was generally a proponent of lightly dressed flies and I have proved their worth time and again. So, on the evening in question, there was no great surprise in this fly doing well – at times it did exceptionally well! The first fish was a modest but lovely six-pounder; the second a cracking sixteen-pounder that fought ferociously. The third was just a grim pull on the fly that did not materialise into a hooked fish. And then, it was dark and the opportunity was over. Two fish may not seem much; it might have been three. But most times down the Cottage stream, I and other rods would have been well-pleased in catching one fish. To get three takes on successive casts was something of a red-letter day! When I got back to the hut, I found in the light of the Tilley lamp that my double hook was well-mangled, a pretty likely contributory factor to my not hooking the third fish. I left the fly with a note for Dennis before leaving the hut that night. I believe a fellow rod saw fit to straighten the hook the following morning and give the fly another try. I am not convinced that was a good idea. Once damaged, is a weakened hook worth repairing?

There is so much more that could be said of Kercock under the watch of Dennis. However, times move on and, as Dennis was always the first to admit, nothing stays the same; things are always changing. When His Lordship passed away, the beat was briefly let through the new Lord Perth but it was shortly to be sold in a deal that amalgamated the upper and lower fishing. Twelve rods were to be administered across the entire beat with options on the Estate fishing an extra rod. This meant for busy fishing with little choice of water; you fished the stretch that you had been allocated on the day. Weekly lets were rapidly becoming a thing of the past, and there was absolutely no guarantee of accessing the best or even adequate water on a one-day visit. The worst aspect for Dennis was that he could no longer guarantee the enjoyment of his rods. Dennis had won the respect and trust of his original employer on the beat. With change of ownership, all that was lost and the arrangements became less assured and more contentious. Things may be different now. However, it was time for Dennis to move on and that was what he did. It was not without regret on his part but, with failing health, it was probably timely that he did so. For many, he left a legacy that is unlikely to be repeated. He strove for the fulfilment of his rods and, for the most part, his loyalty was reciprocated. It did not always work – there are always those with a more selfish agenda – but, for those for whom Kercock became home, the experience was irreplaceable. These are the rods who owe Dennis so much, not just in terms of fishing but on their very perspectives of what makes life worthwhile. Dennis knew tragedy in his own life but details of what he confronted only emerged in conversation over the years. It is not my place to share these details. What I can say is that knowledge of the difficulties Dennis experienced over the years makes his attitude, generosity and friendship all-the-more cherished. He not only taught me things to do with fishing, he taught me a great deal about living.

The Angus South Esk –
A Once Great River

For me, fishing has always been opportunistic. I suppose this reflects how I am as a person. I have planned certain things in my life, probably more so in recent years than previously but, in the main, I have been content to ride the wave and take things as they come. My choice of rivers to fish has been very much in response to what circumstances have offered as opposed to planned expeditions to far-flung places. There have been exceptions but most of my salmon fishing has been in rivers that, relatively speaking, have been on my doorstep. The river South Esk falls very much into this category. It is a delightful stream with a phenomenal heritage. Visit the lodge on Upper Kinnaird and peruse the photographs that line its walls. Be amazed and envious of the spring catches made by Lord Southesk and his favoured guests in the late fifties and early sixties – daily catches of sixty-plus salmon to three or four rods. Check the size of these gleaming fish and be duly awed by the 47-lb springer caught in 1959. Be staggered by how such a modest river could accommodate the 59-lb autumnal leviathan with its sepia stare captured in 1922. Things are, of course, very different now. I recently was party to a 'glory day' when a generous handful of spring fish were caught. In current times, such a catch is quite exceptional. How things have changed for the worse in recent decades. It would be easy and probably misguided to blame recent declines on the excesses of rod catches in past times. A great many things have changed in the past fifty years that have surely contributed to the demise of the Atlantic salmon, things that include the ruthless efficiency of sea- and coastal fisheries, the unbounded explosion of sea-mammal predators in coastal and estuarine waters and the uncertain impact of much that has changed in ocean currents and feeding. It is disconcerting that, in this age of declining stocks where anglers are in the main returning their fish, they should be further targeted with the proposed introduction of a licence-to-kill policy or compulsory catch and release when little action is being taken on many other fronts that have surely had a negative impact on stocks.

My first sorties to the South Esk were by invitation. I first met Vic when I was planning to move to the Mearns in eastern Scotland. He built my house but much more than that, he introduced me to salmon fishing in the area. I am sure Catriona's sense of humour accommodated the inevitability that our builder was also a fisherman but she must have noted with a measure of apprehension that most of our meetings to discuss the build slipped easily into a discussion of fishy things! Be that as it may, we ended up with prompt access to a very fine house. My first outing with Vic was to Lower Kinnaird. We were almost certainly a bit too early in the season to do well because any fish that arrive in the spring tend to keep running until they encounter the weir at the top of Upper Kinnaird. Here they stop, providing what was once a superb early season beat and the site of the unbelievable catches to which I have referred. Later that same year, Vic asked me to accompany and keep an eye on his old friend Willie Begg on the short Powmouth beat. Willie was Vic's journeyman when he first got started as a plasterer in the building trade and it was Willie who helped Vic get a good start in his career. Powmouth is a two-rod beat of little renown. It is a very short channel of only a few hundred metres in length and has only a handful of lies, two of which account for most of its catch. I was excited by the prospect – I always get excited by the prospect of fishing somewhere new. I was warned by Vic to expect two things of Willie. One was that he would want to blether and, if I did not insist otherwise, not much fishing would be done! Secondly, I was to expect Willie to turn up in immaculate attire with all the latest tackle. He did not disappoint on either count. We wandered up to the top of the beat and, sure enough, a very dapper Willie Begg was in fine form recounting tale after tale of fine exploits on the Spey. Eventually, he had a couple of casts at the Slunk, the neck at the top of the run where the beat starts. The river was in beautiful ply, fining down after a considerable September spate. The run just shrieked of fish but it would have been easy to assume that, if they were present at all, the salmon had entered some mean conspiracy of seclusion that involved a complete ban on any visible surface activity. Willie had no sooner got started than he declared it time to retire to the car and eat his lunchtime piece. Well, that was fine but, having checked that he had no serious objection to my continuing, I stayed in place; the stream just looked too good for us to return fishless.

I was fishing a shrimp-type dressing whose gold body and black and orange hackles looked irresistible. The whole contraption positively shone and kicked in the sunlit water, as indeed it had done in a bathtub of water the previous night! (Catriona remains blissfully unaware of much that goes on in the preparation of a good day's fishing!) When the take came, it was a solid pull and the rod bent into something truly substantial. It was obviously a good and heavy fish but it was disinclined to leave the sanctuary of the Slunk channel. Then everything came to a standstill. My trusty Powerlite fifteen-footer was well bent and I could feel the occasional tumbling pulse of the fish but it refused point blank to run. By this time, I was out of the water and had progressed downstream of the fish. I tried changing the angle of strain but to no effect. It slowly dawned on me that the fish may very well have succeeded in snagging my line around some obstruction on the riverbed and that this was preventing it from running. I decided to ease the strain and let the rod straighten slowly. Then I felt for the fish again by raising the rod tentatively, fully expecting to feel the combined weight of fish and some cruelly shaped log or branch. Not so! With one almighty rush, the fish stripped me to the backing and was rapidly heading down the pool as if intent on getting back to the salty environs of Montrose Basin. The fight was well and truly on! I must have played the fish, strong runs up and down the pool and mostly at the far bank, for some fifteen minutes before Willie reappeared. His timing was perfect because landing this fish on my own would have been a major challenge, there being no obvious place to beach a fish in this high water. We did have a net so, despite Willie's reservations about his ability to hold and lift the fish, I decided that netting was our only chance of success. Now Willie was of slight frame and he was not in the best of health, his earlier work having taken toll of his lungs. I had severe misgivings about how this whole episode might culminate but, having made all the appropriate mutterings about how I would not manage this on my own and that if we lost the fish it would not matter (if only!), I eased the fish across the waiting net. When Willie lifted the net, I knew the fish was in the bag but it was not at all certain that Willie, let alone the fish, would end up on the bank. There was no way Willie was going to get net and fish back up the grassy slope without assistance, so with complete disregard for his very fine jacket and his general wellbeing, I grabbed Willie by the collar and dragged him, net and fish unceremoniously up the slippery banking. I only stopped when we made the flat edge of the wooded margin! If Willie was taken aback by this rough treatment, he did not show it. We were both amazed at the size and beauty of the fish. It was spanking new from the sea and its gleaming silvery flanks were liberally spattered with long-tailed lice. What a beauty! I kept that fish and, when weighed later that evening, it proved to be a couple of ounces short of twenty pounds. It was my first fish from the South Esk and, to this day, is my best from the river. As things stand, I doubt very much if I shall catch anything bigger from this or any other beat of the South Esk. It is salutary to think that Lord Southesk and his cronies, only some few decades previously, would not have batted an eyelid at the capture of such a wonderful fish – a fish that, for them, would have fallen into the category of good but normal.

Having been introduced to this lowest of stretches on the Kinnaird fishings and having tasted the excitement of success there, it is perhaps not surprising that I should have returned to the beat on many occasions over the past fifteen years. It has never yielded a fish quite in the category of my first success, although it has come close. I got into the way of making short (often early morning or evening) visits when I thought the water and prospects would be good. I paid attention to tide times and, when water levels, tides and weather coincided, had considerable success. Initially, this meant being on the alert and making a quick sortie to the Estate office the day before an intended early start. Unless the river was in spate, it paid to fish when the sun was off the water. Today, river conditions and rod availability can be checked and bookings made online, something that has made fishing much more accessible to a great many people. When the late summer grilse were running, this was a great place to be. A small rod sufficed and sport could be fast and furious! There came a time when, if anything can be guaranteed in fishing, I could arrive on the water and expect to catch some of these lively fish; it was very rare to go home without one. The biggest impediment to success was being over-eager on the strike. There was always a real temptation to strike on seeing or feeling the take and this would invariably result in missed fish or fish that were lost in the ensuing fight. My most successful tactic was to cast and get the line in order and then turn my attention away from the stream. It may sound crazy but it was effective; try it if you are not convinced! I would adjust the ratchet on my reel to a light setting – not too light or you get overruns – and let the fish pull and hook itself off the reel. All I did subsequently was to lift the rod into the fish clamping the line with my fingers against the rod handle. Easy but nerve tingling! I suppose casting then closing your eyes to the world – quite literally – might have the same result. At least, with my approach, I could still commune with the birds and trees as I waited in keen expectation for the inevitable almighty pull. It was all very exciting stuff.

Although there were only a couple of reliable lies on the beat, this did not matter when there was only one rod fishing. One year, a further holding spot appeared when a large broadleaf trunk fell across part of the river in the middle of the beat. This proved to be a real attractor for grilse; they loved it! Where once the water flowed sedately without feature, there was now a discernible push from the sunken branches and, no doubt, a measure of cover and shade. I caught grilse all around this obstruction but the fish seemed to have a distinct preference for gathering immediately upstream of and hard against the fallen crown. They would take with gusto straight off the tide. I benefitted on several occasions from this unexpected bonus lie and then, just as suddenly as it had appeared, it was gone. Sandy, who looked after the water at that time, explained that complaints had been made to the effect that the banks were not being maintained and that fallen timber was not being removed from the river. He felt obliged to clear the offending obstruction and, indeed, it was his job to do so. Such is fishing; fishermen are all different and have varying expectations as to what makes a good beat. It may not have suited everyone but, for me, the bonus lie certainly was good while it lasted!

When I first started salmon fishing, wading was never a problem. It was all a matter of being confident but not over-confident. The transition from thigh- to chest waders was easy and appropriate to accessing lies in a way that offered a chance of success. Wading in deep water is not a problem as such; it is the speed of water and the nature of the riverbed that merit care and attention. There is buoyancy associated with deep wading that is at once easy and exciting. Once you know the riverbed, you can feel for and touch down on familiar stones and boulders, all the while feeling relaxed, buoyant and light on your feet as you progress downstream. This contrasts with rushing water and unknown obstacles that can make wading decidedly tricky even in relatively shallow water. However, over the years, my mobility and balance became poorer and, although I did not realise it at the time, I was heading for a hip replacement that eventually became a double replacement. I was pretty determined to make a full recovery from this ailment with the uncompromising intention of regaining the mobility and physical confidence of my youth; there seemed no point in setting my sights too low! My first operation was several years ago in early April and, after a couple of months, my recovery was such that any lack of full mobility was in no way hampering my work activity. At this juncture, I reasoned that, if I was fit enough to work, then I was fit enough to fish and, crucially, fit enough to wade. This may not have been an entirely logical conclusion but I was in no mood to analyse it further; the river seemed to be beckoning. As things transpired (water, weather, tides and the like), I first tested the wisdom of this assumption about work and fishing at Powmouth during the first week of June. It was interesting, to say the least, to negotiate the descent of the vertical ladder from the upturned railway girder that served as a bridge. This was the easy access to the beat that avoided a tortuous walk up the side of a neighbouring field. Having carefully negotiated the bank-side walk, I arrived at the top end of the beat and it was looking great. As it happens, I had come equipped to fish for sea trout. This, to my way of thinking, was not unreasonable. The spring salmon run was surely over and it seemed a bit too early to expect grilse. Moreover, June and July were the months for sea trout. Accordingly, I was fishing a couple of flies (small Cascade and Silver-Jungle-Stoat, no doubt) off my preferred single-handed rod for sea trout. Everything went swimmingly well until I hooked something – and 'something' turned out to be a lively salmon of about seven pounds. It was strong but eventually tired sufficiently that I could ease it on to the small sandy spit at the top of the run. This was always the preferred place to beach a fish, assuming the water was not too high, in which case the spit would be well and truly submerged. Well, there it was – a new-run silver beauty. All that remained was for me to grasp it by the wrist of its tail and slip the hook from its mouth. Now, the one thing you cannot do readily or wisely in the weeks and early months following a hip replacement is to bend down. Try asking a scarecrow to kneel in a field and it will continue to give you a blank stare! I tried bending the 'good' leg and tried to maintain a straight body from shoulder to ankle on the 'bad' side. The result was a sort of balletic pose of which my daughter Eilidh (being a dancer) would have been proud! The fish obviously tired of the acrobatic show because it promptly shed the hook, flapped its tail and returned to where it belonged. Not to worry, it was encouraging that there were fish to be caught – or thoughts to that effect! The very next cast and salmon number two was hooked. This one was slightly smaller but at least as determined as it its neighbour to resist capture. It tore upstream before shedding the hook. Well, you must be philosophical about these matters. Fish are lost on occasion and this one would probably only have weighed about five pounds. It is truly remarkable how you can rationalise defeat in adversity! Salmon number three was identical to the second in one respect but different in others. It took on the very next cast – that is the similar bit – but it differed in being much bigger than the other two. Well, this fish, reminiscent of its autumnal peer that I encountered on my very first visit to the beat, had only one thought in mind – to get back to sea as quickly as possible seemed to be the order of the day! It ripped twenty yards of line and thirty yards of backing as it rushed downstream on the far bank, then stopped momentarily before continuing its desperate rush. I was surprised to see an enormous tail and back surface on the inside water some seventy yards from where I stood. The fish had crossed over to my bank as it raged downstream. Given my fragile state of recovery, there was no way that I could clamber on to the bank and run downstream. Then it shed the hook. I had to laugh; it was either that or to cry! It is not often that I have had three salmon take on three successive casts. All in all, perhaps I was not quite ready for three unexpected salmon. But I have no regrets; I knew at the time that I had the making of a story. My friend Doug was amazed that, after losing the first fish, I had not gone back to the car to fetch my double-handed rod and other salmon gear. He sort of missed the point about the Herculean effort that was required to get there in the first place! I suppose my final thought on the matter is that I was glad that none of my 'team' (general practitioner, surgeon and physiotherapist) was there to witness the event. I doubt if they would have approved of my unbounded enthusiasm and stupidity.

Powmouth is precious. I guess we all have a favourite fishing place and, certainly at one time, Powmouth was that place for me. This may still be the case. It is not easy for me to ascertain why this should be so. Powmouth is short and, in the main, lacks features. But it has hidden gems that contribute to its place in my affections. I know – or knew – its riverbed much better than I know most of those on the beats I fish. I got to know its wildlife. In fact, there were times when I became an accepted part of the scene. I used to meet otters regularly. They have even swum and stopped within rod length, one in front of me, the other behind, with heads raised as if enquiring of my luck. They seemed to accept me as a harmless addition to their territory. True, most of the time, I could hardly be accused of decreasing the fish stocks. But I did catch fish and sometimes a lot of them with some very good ones included. I have fished Powmouth throughout much of my development as a fisher of salmon and, in a strange way, this small beat has become an acquaintance; it has assumed a personality in my experience. I have shivered in its mists on early September mornings and I have stood enthralled by its spell in the warmth of a June evening. I think it may still have a lot to share with me if only I would return to its banks. I must do so. If I knew that my next cast was to be my last, I would happily wish myself at Powmouth when conditions were right.

The reason that my trips to Powmouth became less frequent was that another opportunity to explore part of the South Esk came my way. Again, this was through the generosity of Vic. When I first met him, Vic was both farmer and builder. This combination of interests meant that he was well-known and well-connected round and about Angus and the Mearns. It was also known to many that he enjoyed fishing and it was through his network of acquaintances that the opportunity to rent fishing at Justinhaugh arose. Lower Justinhaugh used to be ticket water with permits available through the hotel beside the iron bridge above Tannadice. Things have changed. The hotel has closed and, although the fishery has remained under the same ownership, it has subsequently been leased on an annual basis to tenants. In typically generous fashion, this meant that Vic, who had very little time to fish himself, encouraged his friends to have a cast. A few people, including myself, were thrilled to pursue this offer of fishing. I used to phone Vic in advance of any visit to the beat and he always gave enthusiastic encouragement with the proviso of keeping him informed of any success. From the outset, I suggested to Vic that he might encourage my friend Dennis to become involved. Dennis had just retired from his position as ghillie at Kercock on the Tay and it was obvious that his experience could be invaluable in maintaining and improving the Justinhaugh fishery.

Potentially, Justinhaugh is a lovely piece of water. It is mostly fished from the left-hand bank and extends from the pool above the iron bridge to where the Bog Burn enters at Tannadice approximately one and a half miles downstream. However, it is a beat that has suffered from neglect over many years. No doubt this was of less consequence in the bygone years of 'plenty' but, in today's scenario of diminished runs, restricted bank access and encroaching vegetation have added to the challenge of successfully encountering fish. During the first three seasons, it was very much a case of opening a bank through judicious strimming and clearance of debris to enable access. It was a case of lopping branches and tree felling to enable a cast (and landing of fish) in different water heights as well as the careful and selective removal of branches so that likely casts could be made without undue removal of bank-side cover. This had obviously been done in times past as evidenced by coppiced alder and willow along the riverbanks but it had not been done in recent years. The ravages of time were evidenced by much more than tree neglect. The beat was littered with great lengths of rusted scaffolding from a time when the iron bridge had been under repair. Apparently, the whole network of scaffolding was ripped off the bridge in a heavy storm. Much of this has now been removed but new pieces of scaffolding continue to be exposed on the riverbed following heavy spates. Cement blocks and brickwork from previous sluices are littered throughout the beat. Many of these but not all have now been removed. Vast downstream movements of gravel are a common feature throughout the South Esk and Justinhaugh seems particularly susceptible to major shifts in its river bed through gravel accumulation. Although the riparian rights ensure access, adjacent landownership is not confined to the owner of the fishings. This has resulted in unexpected and inexplicable felling of trees to the potential detriment of the fishing asset. One year, it also led to the sudden and unwelcome placement of a traveller community beside one of the most productive stretches of water. This led to uncontrolled poaching – not all by rod – during the key sea-trout months of June and July. It also led to unmanaged bank-side erosion by horses and extensive littering throughout the beat's length. To all these problems, must be added the rampant invasion of giant hogweed and Himalayan balsam along the banks. To top it all, the whole South-Esk rod fishery had essentially collapsed in face of, amongst other things, a destructive coastal net fishery.

So why bother pursuing this fishery if things were as bad as I have outlined? Well, I and one or two others were fishing by invitation through Vic's generosity, so a bit of bank-side clearance seemed the least we could do; ultimately it could only be to our own benefit. It was also a fishery that I could class as local being some twenty miles from where I live. A mild evening with good water, a quick word with Vic, and I could be on the river within thirty minutes. In fishing terms, ready access at key times is all important. So, although the banks were in dire need of improvement, I could access the few stretches that were fishable at virtually anytime and be confident of being the sole rod on the beat. That is a wonderful recipe for success anywhere, assuming some fish are running and settling in a beat and, of the few pools that were fishable in these first years, some of them proved to be real gems! The beat was lightly fished which meant that the season's total was never going to be large. Twenty fish was about average, with the best quality fish in terms of size and appearance being caught in the late spring and early summer. Autumn fish were relatively numerous but smaller and often dark in readiness for spawning. By the third year of Vic's tenancy, I could time my sorties to Justinhaugh and be sure of catching something. I was getting to know the lies and how fish might be tempted from them. Most of the time, I was on my own and that year we had nearly thirty fish. This may seem a meagre total to those who can remember the days of plenty from previous decades but, given the state of the beat and its low rod pressure, it represented good fishing.

Thanks to Vic, I spent many absorbing hours on the banks at Justinhaugh. However, it became apparent that he was unlikely to continue with his tenancy given his lack of opportunity to fish. At this juncture, I took over the tenancy on the understanding that a small syndicate would be formed to help pay the annual costs. It seemed a reasonable move given the amount of bank-side work that I and others had done over the previous few seasons; it would have been galling to have left the beat and all our efforts at improvement without reaping some reward. Things have, of course, changed. What was, in recent years, a virtually unfished water has become a small-club water which, although not heavily fished, does get much more attention and rod pressure than previously. Arguably, this is good for the beat and should have allowed some realisation of its potential. It might be expected that catch totals would have increased but this has not been the case. In recent years, the season total for salmon has remained stubbornly around the twenty-fish mark; sea trout numbers have improved and, in total, often match those of salmon. So why have the catches not increased in response to fishing effort? There is, of course, no simple or definitive answer but I suspect that the salmon are just not there in sufficient numbers to populate the beat beyond a few key lies. When I was virtually the sole rod on the water, I had regular access to these lies. Today, others share this opportunity and have a measure of success. In the main, it is the rods who fish most that have had most success. Last season, I had very little success despite trying to time my efforts with favourable conditions. I suspect there are not enough fish to go around and those salmon that are present and resident soon become wary of our efforts. Over the years, we have landed some good fish but nothing spectacularly large, with our biggest being in the region of eighteen pounds. Our best fish are generally in the earlier season and some beautiful springers of fourteen- to sixteen-pound weight have been caught. There have been days of three or four fish and days when more should have been landed. Some of my most memorable tussles from the time of Vic's tenancy were with summer grilse. They can fight so hard! I recall one fish that I hooked in the favoured Red Brae pool that positively tore upstream and seemed intent on pushing on through the white water and into the pool above. At one point, I had the distinct impression of the fish being uphill of me! Eventually, it was netted back in the main body of the pool where I had stood throughout the fight. Unfortunately, these grilse have been in very short supply in recent seasons.

Autumn fishing at Justinhaugh can be good but the fish are invariably coloured. I am not at all certain where these fish come from but pools and streams that seemed devoid of fish in August and September can be alive with splashing residents in October. Perhaps they have been hanging around the estuary at Montrose Basin or perhaps they have moved upstream from the holding water of the Finavon beat. They may even have slipped downstream from the water above Justinhaugh in search of spawning gravel. Whatever, some of them are heavy. Last year, I hooked and landed a fine fish of twelve pounds on a tiny Stoats-Tail double. The fight was short and hectic on the single-handed rod I was fishing in low water. For days, I had the friction burns on my fingertips to remind me of a screaming reel and tearing line. A week later, I lost a heavier fish on the double hander. I played that fish hard for twenty-five minutes before the line 'pinged' and I removed tail- and dropper flies from the branches of a bankside tree. I saw the long back and the spade-like tail of this fish on two occasions but have no idea what it weighed; it was certainly heavy!

Things are somewhat different when it comes to sea trout. In previous years, numbers had become dreadfully depleted when compared with the glory days for which this river was renowned. However, in the past couple of seasons, the expectation has been that coastal nets should not kill sea trout and, perhaps because of this, sea trout numbers have stabilised and may indeed be increasing; time will tell. What is undoubtedly true is that the quality of sea trout being caught is excellent. Strong, clean fish, in the two- to three-pound class can be caught regularly throughout June and July and virtually no fish are caught that are less than one pound in weight. So, this is a real asset. Indeed, one of the joys in fishing the beat has been to share sea-trout experiences with other rods. It is often very unpredictable but most of the rods have experienced evenings when the fish have been moving and glimpses have been afforded of the river's potential. The tackle is light and the flies are small – tiny Pearly Stoats and Dark Mackerels being trusty favourites. Bill Currie was a great advocate of the Dark Mackerel. Why its magenta body and hackle with darker wing should be of any use in near darkness is beyond me but it is a real winner and I would think my chances of success much depleted if I did not have a few in my box. The takes, when they come, can be sudden and aggressive and the fight is invariably strong and exciting in the semi-darkness of a June night. I have had fish tear down the length of a pool before crashing around on the surface as I put the brakes on the rush and ease the fish back to where I stand. On these occasions, everything is dark and uncertain. The river changes character and trees and bushes seem to have shifted position. Even the water noises seem different. I hear sounds that I had previously missed. And then, the fish approaches the waiting net. The water breaks as I ease the fish over the rim of the net, trying to catch a glimpse of its trajectory in a glimmer of dull light and all the time praying that the dropper will not snag. If it is not the net, then the edge of my wader or even the sole of my boot can be the snagging point – yes, the latter has happened with the inevitable result! And then, the lifting of the net and the astonishment at just how heavy the fish feels. The small surface 'vee' as it approaches the net always seems to belie the size of the fish. These fish are wonderful trophies and most of them are returned. On a good night, three or four will have been landed and at least as many will have been lost. The next evening may yield nothing. Such is sea-trout fishing. I look forward immensely to seeing how things develop on the sea-trout front in the coming seasons. I wonder if we shall return to the glory days. I do, of course, hope that the salmon fishing will improve but, if nothing else, a vibrant sea-trout prospect would entice me to maintain the tenancy.

So, there we have it – the challenge of a once majestic but now depleted South Esk. I want to keep going with Justinhaugh in the hope that things will improve. At times, it is a very tough call. It only takes one storm and spate or some thoughtless action by a bank-side owner and we seem to have taken a step back. It is a beat that I want to love and cherish but, strangely, I still have not felt truly at home on its banks. I hope that will change. Its banks are full of life. Wagtails, dippers and kingfishers abound and finches, robins and wrens are always busy. Herons fish in stately fashion and otters do their nightly thing. But there always seems to be some material or aesthetic impediment to its full enjoyment. It is difficult to pinpoint exactly what detracts from its potential majesty but I suspect that it has something to do with a growing awareness that the whole stretch shows such signs of wear and tear; on occasions, the whole place just seems so incredibly tired and jaded. The uncertainty of much that is mooted within the Fishery Board is also a source of some considerable disquiet. Would I continue to fish if 'catch and release' for all migratory stock became compulsory throughout the entire season? I do not know but I think I might well curtail my efforts.

Through all of this, the support of our beat proprietor and fellowship of other rods have become essential parts of the scene and, in this regard, my friendship with Doug has been central. Doug has become inextricably linked with my experience of the South Esk. I could not wish for a more generous and helpful companion on the riverbank. Doug is a principled and resolute man. There was a time when he would not go near the Angus Esks because of the very mixed and ambiguous messages and interests of the Board regarding rod- and net fisheries. Eventually, he saw sufficient light in the offing that he was tempted back, not least by my repeated invitation to have a cast at Justinhaugh. Doug knew this water from the times of day permits through the hotel, so his perspective on the river and its fishing is interesting. Nobody works harder at trying to clear and maintain the banks than does Doug. But his efforts go far beyond issues of access. He takes delight in the success of others and is always the first to make way for another rod when a pool is to be fished. If you are short of a rod or a line or a couple of flies, then Doug is your man. I suppose he and I are quite different as fishers. I tend to favour longer slower rods and longer line heads; Doug is all about slightly shorter, lighter and faster rods with shorter line heads. Doug will have a range of flies, indeed numerous boxes of assorted flies; I shall appear with a couple of Cascades and Stoats, perhaps of different sizes. I travel light; Doug travels heavy! I guess he is covering 'eventualities' as he might see them. It is a source of continued fond amazement to one and all just how much tackle Doug will take to the river. But then, which one of us who has fished with Doug has not benefitted from the present or loan of rods, lines and flies when on the river bank? How many fish, that might otherwise have been lost, has Doug netted for fellow anglers? It does not stop with tackle. You can guarantee that Doug will have packed an extra lunch or two just in case a fellow rod should prove 'needy'. I recall travelling with Doug to fish in Norway when, in the airport transfer lounge he produced packed lunches for each of his seven companions! He has helped me through times of restricted mobility when wading and clambering around riverbanks has been far from easy. Indeed, he made repeated visits to my house and helped me in the days immediately following both hip replacements. You cannot ask much more of a friend. Once you have been with Doug on the river, you quickly realise that he is a great fisherman. We fish in quite different manners. Suffice to say that Doug catches fish. If he were to leave our syndicate, my enthusiasm for keeping things going would be much diminished. Perhaps Doug epitomises more than anyone else the assertion – if I may be granted leave to lean on the oratory of grand politics – that we should be asking not what the river can do for us but rather what we can do for our river. Arguably, no river is more in need of such generosity of spirit than the once glorious South Esk.

The Angus North Esk – Dreamlike
Banks of Balmakewan

For most of the time I have been fishing the South Esk, I have also had access to a week's fishing on the North Esk. As with Justinhaugh on the South Esk, my introduction to the North Esk was through Vic. He had secured the tenancy for a week in late August at Balmakewan and extended an invitation to myself for the week. He also extended this invitation to several other rods who fished when they were available to do so. Often, this would be confined to first light in the very early morning and perhaps again in the evening. What a privilege; what a joy to fish this water.

Balmakewan is a most beautiful piece of water with a long history of great escapades. Have a look at the fishy pictures in the 'hut' (which is a well-appointed lodge for the use of fishing tenants). There are several of well-known characters happily posing with their spring and autumn 'trophies', not all from the very-distant past. There is certainly ample photographic evidence adorning the walls to whet the appetite. And then, take a stroll along the banks. The streams and pools look great and you will almost certainly see fish; you cannot ask for much more before your first cast. On a desert island, if you were to close your eyes and drift your way on to some dream-like fishing, you might well find yourself on the banks of Balmakewan.

The beat is fished from the left-hand bank. Balmakewan is downstream from Inglesmaldie and above Gallery. At the very top of the beat, the right-hand bank is fished by the Pert rods; the rest of the right-hand bank is fished by Gallery rods. The top of the beat features the very productive (and sometimes busy) Luther pool where the Luther water pours into the main river. The confluence of the two streams at the head of the beat forms a rapid cascade of water that eases into a very long and (in most heights) sedately flowing pool. At times, a lot of fish lie in the fast water of the Luther pool before running upstream to

Inglesmaldie and beyond. Fish are present throughout the pool with different stretches fishing better than others at different water heights. It contains some fairly substantial ledges (a feature of the North Esk). The pace quickens at the very tail of the pool (the Stobbs outside the lodge windows) and then there is a rush of white water into the neck of the Island run. The rushing stream of the Island opens into the Arn with its glides, short aprons and enticing ledges; again, ledges are an important feature. If the water is not too high, this is a great spot for fish to stop before proceeding to the Luther. On its day, the Island stream is a real gem. The glides of the Arn are mostly smooth with a few telling interruptions near the far bank. At certain heights, these glides can look a bit shallow and featureless but that is deceptive. Locally, there are some deeper channels and some very good lies that merit a careful approach. And then, the whole river pours into the neck of the glorious Red Braes pool. What a gem! If Red Braes was the only pool on the beat, for my money, it alone would be worth the ticket! Where and how to catch fish in this pool depends very much on water height. In the past couple of seasons, it has changed in character. A few years ago, it fished unusually well throughout its entire length, including the very enticing glide at its extreme tail. It changed in character following the record flood levels of a recent winter and two years ago, it did not fish as well – at least for me – as previously. I suspect this will be a temporary decline in its fortunes as new lies become established. (Indeed, last year, it fished spectacularly well.) Then there is the rapid neck of the Laird's Cast. Fish will lie in this fast water but there are other taking spots as the glides develop downstream and again in the deeper dub towards its tail. The Laird's Cast is not always the easiest and most productive stretch but it is fascinating fishing. One year, I fished it almost to the exclusion of more easily accessed water and it was a great experience. I suspect that it is a pool that would repay a bit of imaginative fishing; how to get the fly down and fishing in the fast neck and how to entice fish from the slower dub and quickening apron at its tail. The tail can fish well with plenty of grilse being caught on small flies. The apron then spills into the neck of the Upper Gallery. I suspect that this pool fishes much better from the right-hand bank. It does produce fish for Balmakewan rods but I have not persevered and cracked the code for success; there are easier and more enjoyable casts from the Balmakewan bank. Finally, there is the Lower Gallery, perhaps the longest pool on the beat. It has an interesting stream in its neck pushing from the far bank before it slides easily into a deep and rather featureless glide. I have had little success here but other rods have done better. I know that I have not given it due attention. Low rod pressure has been such that I have concentrated on what, for me at least, has been more attractive water in the upper parts of the beat. Perhaps it would be a salutary, if somewhat daunting, lesson if I was instructed to fish Lower Gallery to the exclusion of all else. So, there we have it. Balmakewan comprises a good mile of prime fishing and it has been mine to roam and explore for a week over many seasons. Fishing does not come much better than that!

I mentioned that many rods were confined to early morning and evening fishing. This was because Vic extended his offer of fishing to many of his workforce and the Balmakewan week did not coincide with their normal holiday break. It was also true that many of those invited had little rod experience. But what a great opportunity to learn and experience the thrill of fishing! A lot of the rods opted for spinning because this is what came easiest to them. The prize spot was at the top end of the beat on the Luther pool and, on occasions, it proved to be fantastically productive. The preferred approach was to fish a Flying-C upstream, casting into the push of water coming out of Inglesmaldie where it joined the Luther. The key thing was to keep in contact with the bait and the taking spot was often as the bait turned on coming level with the rod. Casting was almost uphill at this spot and the takes would be solid and often from a better class of fish. There were some spectacular catches of fish, often in the twelve- to fifteen-pound class. These fish were often sea-liced and I think they may have travelled freely through the beat but held station, at least for a short while, in the white water at the Luther before progressing further upstream. I recall one catch of three fish before daybreak proper to an inexperienced rod, all of them in the teens of pounds in weight and all of them brand-new from the sea. The majority (but not all) of the fish caught on the spinner were at the junction of the two streams. Some were caught over the ledges a bit downstream of the junction.

Every year, Vic's August week had the stamp of sociability and good fun. It was run for the benefit of many of Vic's employees and friends. Partly because of the inexperience of some rods and partly due to pure chance, there were often a lot of bizarre (and sometimes hilarious) happenings. The time Vic had the 'privilege' of netting a fish with two nets can hardly be forgotten. In helping Dennis net a fish outside the lodge, the first net that Vic used was found to have a large hole through which the fish, still attached to the lure, swam away strongly. Vic was promptly dispatched for a second net and, when forthcoming, the fish was duly netted with Dennis holding both rod and original net. As usual, Dennis took a matter such as this in his stride. He had seen most things on his Tay beat but I think this may have been a 'first'! Then there was the time when Vic enthusiastically plunged down the steep bank upstream of the hut to net a fish for one of his rods. The captor was so excited on receiving the netted fish from Vic that he retired from the river bank and left Vic stranded beside the near vertical bank face. I believe that once the fish was successfully dispatched somebody eventually went to Vic's rescue! All in all, this was happy and successful fishing. It was a real bonus for Vic that he could share this with rods of less experience and I am sure that he got a lot of pleasure out of their success. Having completed the early morning shift, most rods would then depart for the day's work with a possible return in the evening.

I was in the fortunate position of being able to take some holiday during the week which meant that, on some occasions, I was either alone on the beat or would share it during the daytime with only one or two rods. Because the early morning spinning was virtually confined to the Luther pool, the rest of the beat was pretty much left to me. This was a fantastic opportunity where, for most of the time, I would be first rod through several pools on any one day. I too, always started early; normally all rods were on the water by half-past five in the morning. (This was a remarkable achievement in itself, given the social that generally went on in the hut during the preceding evening and well into the night.) I got into the way of starting at the Island run and working my way downstream. Depending on the water height and tides, the Island can be tricky. Fish do stop in the neck of the Island stream but, if the river is high, I think most fish push on to the Luther pool. So, in higher water, it is very much a case of being in place to intercept travelling fish that may pause before making their next run. There are distinct taking spots in the fast water at the neck of the Island and in the small aprons of the Arn where the river widens. All these spots provide transitory opportunities of taking a fish when the run goes through. In my experience, the fish arrive in 'pods', often indicating their presence by oncoming splashes from the lower pool. If you are in the right place at the right time, sport can be spectacular. Others and I have been into two or three fish in rapid succession before things would become relatively quiet. There are of course resident fish in this pool – indeed in all the Balmakewan pools – but they are not necessarily easy to tempt. The real prize is contacting the newcomers and it therefore pays to be alert and watch for their arrival. If the water is slightly lower, as for example when fining down a couple of days after a spate, then fish may pause for some time in the Island stream. I recall one occasion when I hooked and landed two fish in quick succession on the fly. I was not doing anything different from what I had been attempting earlier in the day but quite unexpectedly, a pod of fish had moved towards the neck of the Island. I was on my own when I played these fish and was pleased to beach them successfully. They were both in their teens, one of them very close to twenty pounds in weight and they were both brand new from the sea. These are the fish of dreams. Other fish had been showing at the Island so, at that moment, it remained a very good prospect. The week had been quiet up to that point and I knew Vic was on the water upstream. I therefore raced upstream suggesting that he come down immediately for a cast. Within ten minutes, he was covering the lies but to no avail. I suspect that, in the intervening minutes, the pod had moved on. Perhaps he would have been better off remaining at the Luther pool in the hope of intercepting one on the spinner but I so wanted to see him with success on the fly. Such is fishing in general but particularly so in the Island stream. You take your chance and with a bit of luck your time will come! In more recent seasons, Vic has succeeded well with the fly at the Island and has had some tremendous tussles with strong grilse on the single-handed rod.

I suspect that presentation of the fly in the Island stream can be crucial, with the fly fishing at sufficient depth in the neck being important. This can be tricky and may involve changing flies and tips, perhaps even lines, as you move slightly downstream on to the Arn. Fishing too deep here means inevitable snagging on ledges and boulders, the very features that make this such a productive place. A few seasons ago, my friend Les managed to cut through the race in the neck sufficiently to hook and land a couple of good fish. On a previous occasion, I saw him lose a very good fish that managed to snag his line on one of the ledges. He knew the danger and had waded out, holding the rod high in the hope that the tippet would not fray but, alas, all to no avail. He had done well to hook the fish and I am not sure what else he could have done to prevent the loss.

Changing the fly from something heavy with plenty of presence to something smaller and lighter as you progress from the neck of the Island to the Arn can be crucial. Failure to do so inevitably means snagging on one of the many ledges. It is tempting to keep the heavier fly moving at depth across the ledges and it can be effective but invariably the hook will eventually snag. I learnt this the hard way and the experience was painful – quite literally! I was fishing an intermediate line and a one-inch copper tube. Everything felt good and the fly was coming round nicely but the inevitable snag occurred. I was frustrated because a near-surface fly on the floating line tended to skid and skim much too quickly for my liking. I pulled on the line to no effect and, with a good measure of irritation, pulled hard for a break on the taut line. I did not get the break that I expected but the fly did come free. When I first came to my senses, one of the remaining barbs on a sharp size-twelve treble was firmly embedded in the septum of my nose! It took me a second or two to grasp the situation by which time the line was running away downstream and I was in real danger of following like a bull with a nose ring on the end of a rope – the joys of fishing! It was not exactly a case of the river running red but I had obviously done some damage. What do you do in these situations? Well, it would be nice to hide and become the invisible man for a few moments. But then, there are fish to be caught, so saving face – quite literally – was hardly the top priority. I knew that Dennis was further downstream (a good quarter-mile as it transpired) and, crucially, I knew that he was familiar with how to dislodge such unseemly jewellery. A couple of seasons earlier, I had followed his instructions and successfully removed a well-sunk barb from his thumb. The hook had been nicely inserted by his dog Joe who had inadvertently pulled the line as Dennis was tightening the knot on a fly. Credit to Dennis, he did not blame Joe! Anyway, with the treble now firmly embedded in my nose, I cut the nylon cast near the fly, reeled in the line and headed downstream to meet my fate. Give him his due, I doubt if Dennis even blinked on my arrival but the twinkle of delight in his eye was unmistakeable. We got the matter sorted with twists of nylon and downward pressure on the shank, all on the count of three – or was it two? So, all ended well. I could return to my fishing and Dennis, of course, had yet another story to be recounted at some choice moment. By way of anecdote to the whole sorry episode, I remember thinking that a drop of antiseptic might not go amiss. For want of anything better, I stuck my nose into a glass of Lagavulin and hoped for the best – I suspect an unusual fate for a truly great malt whisky!

On some occasions, we have had very low water during the August week and I am sure this impedes the movement of bigger fish. Smaller grilse will still migrate although they can be truly difficult to catch. On one occasion, we had fished the beat all week in very low water with hardly any success. As a desperate measure, on the last evening, I tried a worm in the neck of the Island run. First cast produced a small fresh grilse and the next cast saw another one lost. I have no idea how many fish were hidden in that neck but it was a bit of a revelation to get one and then lose another in such quick succession. I stopped at that point because it was now too dark to continue and our week had effectively come to an end. Our normal efforts at fly fishing had been to no avail. Perhaps I should have been persevering in hanging a fly at greater depth in the channel. I have done this on subsequent occasions but only had one solid pull. Or what about a dibbled fly or a Collie stripped across the stream? All these are possibilities and, no doubt, I shall give them all a try. Why not fish the worm? If it had proved so successful on that previous occasion of low water, why not give it try again? Why not indeed! But the worm as with many other forms of fishing has become less acceptable. It should be apparent from what I have written elsewhere that I was formerly a great proponent of worm fishing and I would still love to do more of it. However, times have changed and, on many rivers, it is now either banned or considered to be unacceptable. I am not sure if there is now an outright ban on the worm at Balmakewan but I suspect it might cause unfavourable comment from fishers on the opposite bank if I were to give it much of an airing. Anyway, my preference is normally for the fly so I shall probably just have to find ways of being more successful with it when the fish are proving difficult.

Some of my best catches and memories have come from fishing the magnificent Red Braes. Where you catch fish in this pool depends entirely on water height. In medium to low water, all the fish seem to be nearer the far bank, starting with the fast stream at the neck and progressing down the far channel into the main body of the pool. Even towards the tail, the fish seem to prefer the deeper lies off the far bank. It is then very much a case of getting into position, casting down and across with, for me, at any rate, the emphasis on 'down' and letting the fly work seductively across the far lies. I like to get the fly hanging in the stream and use the rod tip to progressively move it across the lies, often in short, subtle changes of direction. I know that other rods prefer a faster moving fly and they certainly have success. So, it all boils down to preference or taste. I prefer a slow fly, others like to work the fly and make it move more quickly. If the fish are there, my choice of fly tends not to deviate much from my standard Cascades and Stoats. But these are always dressed lightly and I would always want a selection of small sizes, typically size ten, twelve or fourteen low-water doubles.

The importance of a lightly dressed fly was hammered home to me in early sorties at Red Braes when I just could not move fish on slightly fuller dressings. My lack of success was frustrating because fish were occasionally showing in the lies but just would not respond to my fly. In desperation, I put on a very small Cascade double. I removed all signs of tinsel from the wing and tail and removed most of the tail fibres and a lot of the black wing. The result was a very sorry-looking creation, resembling a mostly orange nymph dressing for trout but, on this, I promptly caught three grilse in quick succession. All these were taken in the early morning casting towards the far bank where the rougher water eases into the more sedate flow of the main pool. I remember demonstrating this lie to Vic and, sure enough, as the small bedraggled offering came across the lie, a fish took and was landed to order. Strangely, this lie has not been so productive in recent years and fish have been caught in other parts of the pool, not least its tail which had previously been less productive. I recall one year catching a fish in the very cheek of the white water where it tumbles off some large boulders into the neck of Red Braes. A second fish took in the exact same spot on virtually the next cast. I lost this one because my rod bent savagely into the fish when the line was firmly wrapped around the reel handle! Was I careless? Yes, but it is easily done if you are not concentrating. Subsequently, I have never moved a fish – although others have succeeded in doing so – from this exact spot although I give it a try every year. It is truly fascinating how subtle changes in salmon lies occur from season to season. Success can depend on trying previously less productive spots if the assumed hotspots are not rewarding.

Red Braes can provide an education in how fish-taking spots change with water height. There is nothing unique in this but here the shift in lies can be spectacularly clear. A lift in water will see fish move out of the far channel into lies right across the breadth of the stream and, in very high water at Red Brae, fish can be tight into the relatively quiet water of the near-side (Balmakewan) bank. I remember fishing the worm to good effect, close to the nearside bank, when the water was very high and coloured. Fish were taking the worm tight into the bank and indeed over the normally-exposed grass verges of the stream. I guess there is nothing too surprising about this but it was quite astonishing to locate fish right under the rod tip! A very short cast slightly upstream with an appropriate choice of weight meant that the worm was trundling under the rod tip some two- to three metres from where I stood. Within an hour, I caught several fish but should have landed far more. Every cast seemed to result in a knock as the next fish in line intercepted the worm. These were running fish and it is generally assumed that such fish take the bait (be it fly or worm or whatever) when they pause in their travels. This may be the case in most situations but, on that day, I doubt very much if the fish were taking much of a break. When I felt the knock of a taking fish, I delayed the strike and felt tentatively for the second or third pulse. I could feel the fish and, as was my normal practice, I then lifted the rod, assuming the fish to be under the rod tip and expecting to feel its weight. However, as soon as I lifted the rod, invariably the line would track several metres upstream and, in most instances, the fish seemed to drop the bait. I believe these fish were intercepting the bait as they travelled without any appreciable break in their progress. Had I been a quicker learner, I would have landed more fish by angling my strike upstream. However, by the time I realised this, most of the fish seemed to have passed my stance. For me, this was the nearest that salmon fishing has come to catching mackerel from a passing shoal! Brilliant for a time but the whole experience would be dull if fishing was always like this. Better to have a harder-earned reward if enthusiasm and fascination are to persist. Having said that, it was great fun while it lasted! As soon as the water height started to drop, even by a few inches, the fish seemed to move progressively into mid-stream and eventually into the channel towards the far bank. The North Esk generally drops quickly, so the whole scenario of near-bank to mid-stream to far-channel lies can be experienced within a single day at Red Braes.

The neck of the Laird's Cast is fast and narrow and challenging with the fly. In my experience, the best chance of getting the fly down to the fish is to approach the neck from above and effectively fish downstream. This way, the fly can hang in the stream and be worked progressively across the top lies. This is not always easy because the push of water can be great and wading can be difficult to say the least. However, with care, it can be done in lower heights of water. Having said that, I have never done well with the fly in the extreme neck of Laird's Cast. But fish do lie here, especially in low water. One year, I was tempted to fish the worm in the very neck. Having taken three small red fish in quick succession, I gave up the practice. There just did not seem to be any point in disturbing what presumably was a population of very resident fish that would soon be spawners.

Slightly further downstream is where I have had better success with clean fish in the Laird's Cast. About thirty metres down from the start of the neck there is a lovely lie tight into the far bank where a coppiced willow bush seems to survive from season to season. It can be tricky to fish but if you can get the fly to hang in the pocket beside the bush, there is a good chance of intercepting a clean fish. No doubt, the fish can be of varying size but, in my experience, they tend to range from nine- to eleven pounds. Why this should be, I have no idea but perhaps the fast neck holds back some of the better fish, at least for a short time before they forge upstream. I have never caught anything here as large as I have taken at the Island or as others have caught at the Luther pool. But Laird's Cast does hold some good fish and, when hooked, they fight strongly in the fast stream. I remember one eleven-pounder that tore line off the reel at such a rate that I attempted to brake the drum with my fingers. I got the fish but I also had the 'pleasure' of fishing during the remainder of the day with severely blistered fingers. It proved to be a cracking fish and, if given the opportunity, I would, of course, opt again for the pain!

In its upper reaches, the Laird's Cast has a lovely bank for beaching fish in quieter water, at least in most water heights. This is also true of the Island and Red Braes and is a reasonable consideration if the actual landing of fish is important. On many waters, I have lost as many fish as I have landed; at Balmakewan, I have landed most of what I have hooked. Perhaps that is why I have tended to concentrate my efforts on the Island, Red Braes and the Laird's Cast where the chances of landing a hooked fish are good. Things are less certain further downstream at Upper- and Lower Gallery where the left-hand bank is steeper. Here, netting, rather than beaching, of fish becomes a more likely option. I guess it all depends on how much importance is attached to the actual landing of hooked fish. It is surely poor or, at best, dubious practice to consider a hooked fish as caught (and therefore contributing to the catch return) until it has been landed. And what is meant by 'landed'? Well, perhaps the adage: "Could you have eaten it?" is a salutary definition of a fish landed!

Balmakewan is a lovely piece of water and it has been my privilege to taste something of its bounty for many years. This has mostly been late-summer fishing with the expectation of misty dawns and warm fading evenings by the river bank. I have now taken over the tenancy of Vic's August week and have shared some wonderful experiences with fellow rods. In recent years, I have also secured tenancy for three weeks in the spring and – on occasion – we have done quite well in terms of fish caught. However, the catches at this time of year seem less important. It is just such a joy to fish this beat with fellow rods when everything is so fresh at the start of the year. It can be cold and difficult fishing but the experience is uplifting. Now that the downstream cold-water barrier at Morphie has been substantially breached in recent floods and there are fewer impediments to the upstream migration of fish, I expect fish numbers may improve. What I would give to get a falling river, with some warmth in the air and a run of fish – surely the very stuff of fishy dreams!

A final word on Balmakewan. In the lodge, there is (or certainly used to be) a glass-case fish – a truly stunning autumn fish – that weighed thirty-five pounds. It was caught towards the end of last century and its length can be determined as forty-seven inches. Two years ago, my friend Doug caught a spring fish whose length was measured precisely at fifty inches. A conservative estimate has this fish weighing in excess of forty pounds; being a spring fish, it may have weighed considerably more than that. It was of course returned to the river and hopefully survived to spawn in the latter part of the year. Its capture was witnessed by our friend Tom. I met up with Doug and Tom a few minutes after the escapade and to say that they were in a state of shock is no exaggeration. Tales relating to the capture of this fish are rife and mostly erroneous. In one account, the fish was apparently caught on a Yellow-Belly Floating Devon and its captor had to run the length of the Luther pool before landing the fish outside the Lodge! For the record, it was hooked a short distance downstream of the Luther entry at the spot known as 'White Hut'. It was taken on a Red Floating Devon with bristle trimmings (Doug's creation) and the fight lasted some twenty minutes without Doug ever having to move from the one spot. There was no photographic record but the length was determined with a tape measure as the fish lay flat on a sandy spit by the grass verge. The treble hook released, the fish then made a successful return to the river with the blessing of its captor. Later, on their return to the Lodge, Doug and Tom looked at the fish in the glass case and then at one another. Heads were nodding; Doug's fish was most definitely bigger than the glass-case trophy. Time for the celebrations! Such is the potential – and indeed the reality – of fishing at Balmakewan! I hope it remains so.

Hidden Treasure

I know a river – the magic words! In some of my musings, I have been very explicit in identifying rivers with their favoured streams and pools, likewise lochs and their more productive drifts. Elsewhere, I have been less specific, leaving the reader to speculate on exact locations. There is one salmon stream that for me has become something of a treasure and, for that purely selfish reason, I shall not reveal its identity – at least not explicitly. No doubt, there will be some who can identify the river of which I write; for others, it will remain a matter of speculation.

It is not a large river, being entirely fed (at least in summer season) by rainfall over a very modest catchment. Its small catchment is renowned for being effectively in the rain-shadow of most prevailing weather systems. Hence, when its larger neighbours are in flood, this little river can remain resolutely dry and, from a fishing point of view, difficult. At its estuary, it eases into the salt water of one of the most glorious beaches in Scotland – high blue skies of graded intensity with bars of silver sand and green-blue water. On high tides, the flow in its lower reaches comes to a standstill; on very high tides, the whole estuary is flooded and only the occasional (and somewhat disarming) waving of tussocks and bushes indicates the presence of transiently hidden channels. When this is the case, an incoming tide should be treated with due respect. The casual walker can very easily become stranded – or worse – on a fast-disappearing hummock.

Throughout its course, the river tumbles down in a series of short pools and rapids. During the latter part of the previous century, considerable effort went into the construction of croys and small dams in the creation of longer and deeper runs. The result is a series of stepped pools downstream of the main natural fall, the latter forming a potential cold-water barrier to fish movement in the early spring. The creation of such pools has no doubt resulted in more holding water and better fishing but the overall effect can seem a bit contrived. With time, the rough edges to these workings have become more subdued and the main beats have gradually assumed a more weathered and natural feel. The lower reaches have not been managed to the same extent (although that seems to be changing) as the upper beats. In its lower reaches, you can see the results of glacial drift, raised beach and subsequent, ongoing water erosion in the raw. The banks of the lower river retain a more natural and wilder splash, featuring the incessant loosening of rounded boulders and a tangle of bracken, brambles, gorse and alder. The great advantage of all this vegetation is that it provides cover, allowing you to cast here without spooking fish. It also constitutes a brilliant deterrent to casual poaching because it takes a particularly perverse mind-set to penetrate this woven jungle and its hordes of biting midges. This rough fishing is not to everyone's taste but for others it provides wild fishing at its best. Good management does not always mean manicured banks.

Being a spate river, catches can be very weather-dependent and the seasonal total for dry years will be generally lower than for wet years. However, as with most fisheries, there are factors other than weather that affect rod returns. In years when water levels have been low and fish have not been running, the potential spawning stock has previously been vulnerable to coastal netting. This venture has now been curtailed but it may be some time before the real benefit in terms of fish numbers is reflected in rod catches. Indeed, the imponderable determinants of stock survival at sea and the impact of inshore predators may prove decisive in regulating the returning adult population. In years past, a hatchery facility has been maintained that has provided back-up juveniles when spawning and fry survival may have been less successful. In this regard, efforts have been confined to within-river stock where the release of juveniles has even been matched to reaches of the river that reflect their parentage. To my way of thinking, these efforts seem eminently laudable in maintaining the overall genetic integrity and diversity of a sport fishery and its conservation interests.

In recent years, catches have generally exceeded those of earlier decades. Typically, the annual total of rod-caught fish now exceeds four hundred fish – not a vast number of fish but a very encouraging total given the small number of rods. In better years, the season's total has exceeded nine hundred fish; in leaner years, the annual total falls below the four hundred mark. When fish runs and water levels coincide, catches can be spectacular. One recent year yielded a July total exceeding four hundred and fifty fish. Given that July is mostly grilse time, it seems likely that a similar number to this rod-caught total may have been missed or lost in the fight – such is grilse fishing. This constitutes exceptional fishing, not only in current times but during any past period of rod effort. Today, all fish are taken on the fly and are largely returned; in the past, much of the season's total was taken on the worm and fish were killed.

I heard of this river at a relatively young age, at least in terms of my fishing effort. I knew that my friend Les and others had got summer employment on its banks moving boulders around as part of the 'improvements'. I also had a friend who, on occasion, fished this river with his father but all of this was nearly fifty years ago. In terms of my own acquaintance with the river, I must jump some thirty-plus years in my thoughts, to a time when my son David was first invited to fish on one of the main beats on a couple of occasions. It was David's enthusiasm for the place that fired my interest and, the following season, I secured a week's tenancy in August. Now, August can be a good month for grilse but the fishing is very water-dependent and water levels in this month can be notoriously low. In this regard, my first two visits were no exception. On both occasions, in the days prior to fishing, I watched the weather forecasts with a sense of increasing foreboding. Rain was certainly falling and rivers were in spate elsewhere in Scotland and yet the small catchment in which I was interested remained resolutely dry. Any residual flow was confined to the very necks and occasional tails of streams that, in subsequent years, I found to be fabulous holders of fish. In both these early years, the water level was so low that it fell below the zero mark on the gauge for weeks on end. This poor semblance of a river did have pots and runs and there were certainly occasional splashing fish – mostly stale – indicating that at least some of the stock from the earlier runs of that year had survived the adversity of incessant bright sunshine and tepid water. Presumably, many spring and early summer fish had cleared the falls before these extreme low levels discouraged further fish movement.

To say that success under conditions of extreme drought would require the skills of an indigenous hunter would be to attribute supernatural powers to the otherwise superb skills of such a person. The wise hunter – if still alive – would have stayed his hand and waited for the opportunity of success in plenty. It would not be far off the mark to conclude that a special type of depravity – of which I possess my fair share – would be required to even attempt the capture of fish in these conditions. To clamber around for two weeks in a positive tangle of midge-infested, head-high bracken, brambles and gorse in the hope of some derisory cast at a long-spooked resident is hardly the behaviour of a sane person. A midge net was essential gear, meaning that the depravity of this private hell was experienced with blurred vision. Worse, a sort of dementia ensued, where even the simple act of eating became a nightmare. Have you ever tried, in a fit of absent-mindedness, to ingest the sweaty mesh of a midge net and a bread roll? Not a happy experience! It can of course be alleviated by a good swig of black coffee (assuming you have presence of mind to lift the midge net). In my demented state, such sanity regularly escaped me. Suffice to say that, during these first two years, I fished for twelve scorching summer days for the scant reward of one sea trout and a covering of midge bites and thorn scars of which even the most extravagant tattoo artist would have been proud.

Given the experience of my first two visits, it may seem hardly surprising that I cancelled my booking for the following year. But to do so, almost inevitably invited reinforcement (in the most salutary manner) of that which I knew already, namely that fishing on spate rivers is a most fickle business. There are years of drought and years of plenty and, for the most part, their occurrence is unpredictable. The following year – the year of my cancellation – was (of course) one of phenomenal catches. The total for the month of July was mouth-watering. It was, of course, all down to favourable water heights at the crucial time for grilse runs – and run they most certainly did! So, there I was, frustrated over my lack of previous success and contrite over my sad lack of perseverance, tentatively making enquiries of the letting agents about any possible late cancellations. Not surprisingly, they assured me that this was a most unlikely occurrence but that, in the off-chance of a late cancellation (perhaps they were thinking in terms of client death) my best bet would be to contact the keeper directly. Now it is not always possible to tell if someone is smiling or laughing at the other end of a telephone but I suspect that a large measure of desperation and contrition was sensed in my voice. Whatever, I was assured that cancellations were not on the cards but – and what a glorious 'but' – there was the chance of a couple of rods on the lower water. Fishing on this stretch is very much at the keeper's discretion and access is not readily available. I assured him I was on my way!

I fished on two occasions that year. Both sorties involved day trips with something like nine hours of motoring apiece. It is hardly an overstatement to say that both trips were a bit punishing but they were great in the opportunity they afforded. The first outing was with Dennis. Now, at that time, Dennis was struggling a bit with his fitness so he had to mind his step and could not fish much. I lost three grilse that day, all of them played out at my feet. This river can prove difficult when it comes to landing fish but my main problem was one of agility or, more accurately, lack of it. I had not fully recovered from a first hip replacement and was well on my way to needing a second. The trip was not an unqualified success: Dennis was a bit breathless on the bank and I was unable to bend down and land fish! Not to worry, there would always be another occasion. The second sortie (a couple of weeks later) was with my friend Les. Again, the water was good and we caught fish. Well, Les caught fish – three of four grilse as I recall – and he also lost a couple. On that occasion, I lost five, again mostly at my feet. (It was time to get that second hip replacement – job now done.) In retrospect, I had by this time seen the river in its extremes. I had struggled through days of stifling heat and drought but I had also had glimpses of the river at its best. However, these were early days and Les and I were soon to know that we had only scratched the surface of what was on offer. In later years, we were to explore this water and get to know it much more intimately. On the day of our first trip, I now realise that there were almost certainly more grilse to be caught (at least by Les) in some choice pools and runs, had we but known of their existence. To this day, that first occasion was most probably our best opportunity of an impressive catch. One day, we may encounter the same favourable water and good numbers of fish and hope to do better.

In recent years, I have fished low summer water on this river with some limited success. By 'low', I mean gauge levels of five or six inches. On these occasions, the river has been a very different – albeit quite difficult – prospect from that of years with extreme drought. The river has seemed alive in that the water is less tepid and the riverbed is not covered to the same extent in algal slime with its concomitant nightly demand on limited oxygen supply. Under such conditions, the typical push of a stream in the cool, alder-shaded neck of a pool or in the hastening glide of its tail has been enticing. Les and I now have a regular week in early August. Crucially, I think we work well as a 'team'. We both share the opinion that avoiding disturbance to the water will maximise our opportunities of success. If Les has gone through a stretch in the morning, I have no misgivings about undue disturbance and spooked fish when I visit the same stretch later in the day. I think he experiences the same confidence when visiting water that I have fished earlier on a given day.

We generally fish very differently. Les sort of strokes the water from afar. At first appearance, his fishing effort may seem cursory. He will approach the pool or stream quietly and often keeps some distance from the water's edge.

146

Often, he may place a line across a choice stretch on only three or four occasions – three or four casts down the entire length of good holding water. He fishes fine (light nylon and small flies) and often casts relatively square to the flow, inducing speed and movement to the fly. The takes can be solid and determined. I think fish may often move some distance to his fly. He is then off to the next pool, then the next and so on. In other words, he fishes the water quietly and quickly. He often fishes very small Shrimp tubes or sparsely dressed Collie doubles – all very unassuming in their dressing.

In contrast, I think my fishing may be more akin to that of a predatory heron in that I approach the water quietly then stand still. Mostly, I cast downstream rather than square and let the fly swim and hover in the current. My next cast will be from the same position but I shall have lengthened the line, thus covering new water. I believe the fish see my flies before being frightened by any line splash or shadow. I may have three or four stances in a fishing a pool – similar in that respect to Les – but I shall generally take longer than he does when going through a pool. When a fish takes, I do not think it has necessarily moved far to my fly. I do not think there is any right or wrong in our fishing methods. We both catch fish in low water and have confidence in how each other fish with minimal disturbance. If anything, Les often catches more fish than I do – make what you will of that! Neither of us has spent much time 'dibbling' flies when the water is low but I know this approach can work for the keeper when things are otherwise difficult – and he should know!

On the rare occasions when we get better summer water, our approaches remain much as I have described. However, Les is never slow to change from a full floater or a floater with a slow sink-tip to an intermediate line when the opportunity arises. Unless there is a real push of water, I generally remain with the floater (incorporating a short sinking tip) or even a full floater. We may increase the fly size but not much when the water is higher. I do not actually remember catching a summer fish here on anything bigger than a size-eight cascade double – there again, we do not normally have high water. No doubt, there are occasions when something big and showy – perhaps fished at a bit of depth – would do the job as a summer spate starts to recede but, for me, the summer on this river generally means lowish water and small unassuming flies.

Springtime here is a very different matter and I have been fortunate to secure a week's tenancy in early April. This is on the main rotating beats available through the letting agency. It is wonderful to experience the pristine freshness of the place. Dappled greens and yellow are quickening in bursts of bright sunlight amidst the tired browns and russet of winter. In contrast to the sun-faded tiredness of late summer, there is a bright awakening with urgency and expectation in the air. The place is alive with rushing water and birdsong. Warblers vie with finches, tits and blackbirds in declaring and defending their patch in the tapestry of flushing twigs and ancient rock. The first sand martins can make a frenzied appearance above the grassy edge of embankments and later, that same afternoon, they may be joined by the sweeping of house martins and swallows above the tree clearances bordering the middle reaches. Dippers often flit and bob from stone to stone and a greater-spotted woodpecker is often seen to loop in its characteristically undulating way. The serene heron normally remains nonchalant, only to croak its annoyance at any disturbance, its great wings straining in the endeavour of mostly unnecessary flight. A rare sighting of greenshanks can surprise on the shingle banks and the unexpected goshawk may excite near the Estuary. The first of the golden plovers will arrive just before the start of lambing in the upper reaches and, if your luck is really in, you may see a sparrow hawk nail a wagtail at the Falls. Herds of stags, soon to be dispersed, are seen to ford the river in the peace of an evening. All these happenings contribute to the joy and emerging urgency of a spring day.

Spring here is a glorious time of refreshment in the communion of river and fisher. Along the banks, the push of clear water positively sings and dances in the fresh runs and pools. The rocks at the Falls shine with wet spray and small precarious clusters of yellow primrose seem pitched like curious spectators beside the incessant, deafening thunder of the drop. The very water churns and boils its way through rocky cups and bowls, fashioned by centuries of thrusting water, sculpting ever so slowly but irrevocably the ancient hulk. Here, you can sit in the shelter of a pitted rock face and watch what has been going on for millennia. The sun warms your face or back and you relax from your intention of catching fish. You are cradled sleepily and become a peripheral part of things. But your presence has no more bearing on the resolute eroding process than that of a passing fly or dipper – or indeed that of a transient salmon. This is a good time and place to contemplate the utter futility of so much else that tends to clutter your sense of being and purpose – what you refer to as your life; your laughable insistence on acclaiming short-term motivation and achievement in all that you and your peers might otherwise define as 'progress'. Here is an opportunity to rest awhile in a natural time capsule. Pause and be honest. Be aware and be refreshed! Whatever else you might attribute to the definition of the human state, an ability to marvel, to appreciate a sense of beauty and to wonder why this might be so, are surely central and sobering. If this opportunity should come your way, it is yours to cherish or discard. Such is fishing in general and, not least, the secluded corners of spring on this hidden treasure of a river.

The actual catching of fish, or at least the intention of doing so, is of course important to any spring visit; it is, after all, the essential motivation to the whole effort. In terms of fish, it does not always disappoint. I have fished with Doug when he connected with but lost a fish in the run below the Falls. That same year, I had the good fortune to hook and land a beautiful springer in the late afternoon. It took my fly in the slow push at the tail of an enticing pool. It fought doggedly and hard and, fortunately, Doug was to hand when it came to netting and releasing my prize. I love hanging streams such as the tail of this pool, where there is a push of water from an inward bend on the far bank. The fly can be fished slowly and purposefully, where judicious movement of the rod tip induces a change in swing of the fly; the fish seem to like this too. On a recent spring visit, Les had draws from two fish; the following spring we landed three and lost one – the lost one was very big. I never expect to catch too much on a spring visit but sometimes we do remarkably well. The runs of early fish are not large. Very few fish may run on any one tide but the great thing is that they are appearing – the very harbingers of things to come! If I get one springer in my week, I feel I have done well. To get more constitutes a good year. However, as should be apparent from what I have attempted to convey, an early spring visit here is about much more than the mere catching of salmon.

For me, June is very much an in-between month on this river. It is no longer the time for an early springer but fish can be running, often before the main expected run of grilse. Sometimes they can be large. One day, I fished with Les on the lower water. We both caught a fish – and that was the total for the day. Mid-morning saw me hook something heavy. It was a very solid take and proved to be a fresh cock fish of some seventeen-pounds weight. When not intent on hanging itself from the low branches of alders on the far bank, it fought hard and fast in the stream. I eventually landed this fish on a sand bar – now gone but which once divided this stream – where Les released the hook. What a tremendous fish! It was evening before Les hooked his fish. I was fishing above him and could vaguely make out his occasional silhouette on the downstream horizon. I was unaware that he was playing a fish. It fought him hard the length of the stream before being successfully landed. It was the equal of our earlier fish. A day during the 'in-between' times of spring and early summer does not get much better than that.

Most fish here are caught in the summer months when the fishing can be exceptional. So, what constitutes a typically good summer week on this river? I am thinking here of the prevailing grilse runs during July and August. Obviously, the answer to such a question is, among other things, very water-dependent. It also depends very much on what is meant by 'good'. In this instance, I am thinking in terms of numbers of fish. If the water is low, then a good week for a single rod might be counted on the fingers of one hand. But what if the water is right and the fish are running? Obviously, angling competence and luck – in terms of fish missed and lost – come into play. Very occasionally, I still hear of daily catches from north-coast rivers in double figures for a single rod. I have heard of this recently on the Thurso and I have no doubt it may happen on other north-coast rivers but these catches are exceptional. Double figures for a week to a single rod might more typically be labelled as good. There are always considerations that qualify success. Even when catches might be considered good, a rod might think agonisingly over fish missed or lost, fish that might otherwise have boosted the total. Even a good day or week should have been better!

I think a recent summer visit to our river with Les might qualify as good – certainly in our experience of the water. July had reportedly fished well following rain in the latter part of the month and we certainly expected to encounter fish. The river was falling slowly with about twelve- to fourteen inches on the gauge – a much more encouraging prospect than in previous years.

On Monday, early morning, I reacquainted myself with the path at the top of the lower river. I say 'path' but in truth, the way did not appear to have been trodden for some time. Head-high bracken was the norm and both it and the tangle of brambles ensured the regular snagging of dropper fly and net with the occasional tripping stumble thrown in for good measure! (Reminder: The lower river is most definitely a place to travel light – very light and preferably no net.) Rampant gorse and sprouting alder contributed to the jungle feel. None of this aided progress but eventually there was light – quite literally – at the end of the green tunnel, where I emerged through a tangle of alder branches on to the shingle of the top run. It looked superb – if somewhat black – as I crept my way to its neck and started to lengthen line. I had attached one of Doug's tiny Pearly

Stoats to the tail with a very small, stripped-back Cascade on the dropper – the sort of flies which inspire confidence. I did expect a pull in the stream but it was not forthcoming – not at the neck and neither in the main body nor the left-swing tail of the pool. I did not see fish, which was interesting and slightly thought-provoking but no major cause for concern. Off to the next pool! This, of course entailed a return to the jungle. That is the way of things here. You make your approach with as much patience and good temper as you can muster, have a few casts – with or without result – then return to the joys of the scrub.

Beyond a small dub, the next pool beckoned. For me, it is one of the best on the river. The keeper has confirmed that this delightfully enticing run has no name, so I shall call it the 'Nameless' pool. Although I had no indication of having covered unresponsive fish in the first pool, I decided to change fly. A tiny Thunder-Stoat double that I inherited from Dennis went on the dropper; the Pearly Stoat remained on the tail. The Nameless pool is a true gem. Like the one above, it is hardly more than sixty yards in length. It has a beautiful beach of shingle on the left bank and a shady run under willow and alder on the right bank. At its prolonged tail, it sweeps to the left. Fish generally lie throughout its length in the depths of the shady run. I got my first solid pull of the week just as the line started to swing out from beneath the willow bush halfway down the pool. It proved to be a small, lively hen grilse of about three and a half pounds, taken on the Thunder Stoat. Like all other grilse during the week, it was safely returned and, like all fish we caught, it was fresh but free of lice, indicating that it had been in fresh water for at least a few days. What a joy to get a fish and what an encouragement! My fishing with Les is hardly competitive but it was nice to have something to contribute when discussing the day's catch. What a relief!

For the rest of the morning, my mood was light as I made my way from pool to pool. I felt content and at one with the place as I explored enticing runs and tails with an easy confidence in what I was doing. I could relax and even smile my way through the next thorn barrier. Having had some success, nothing seemed to matter anymore. I got a small wake-up call – a reminder to concentrate – when I struck too soon as a bigger fish took me on the dangle in the top part of a long run. Then I got one below the neck of a run below the long pool – a hen fish of about four pounds on the Thunder-Stoat dropper. I decided to put an even smaller Thunder-Stoat on the tail; fish seemed to prefer the more sombre appearance of the Thunder to that of the flashier Pearly Stoat.

I met with Les when we had a break in the middle of the day. It turned out he had met with similar success, so the week was off to a good start! Later that evening, I got two more in one of the best pools and lost one in the small dub at its tail. They were all on the Thunder-Stoat dropper. And that is essentially how the week progressed – a fish here, a missed fish or a lost fish there. The water slowly dropped from Monday to Wednesday and returns became lower. I got a fish on each of Tuesday and Wednesday and I was pleased with both these fish because of where they were lying. They took me at the very tail of the pool – requiring the sort of cast that seems doubtful because the flies must surely be swept into the rush of white water below the tail. Right on the very lip of the tail, the fish latched on to the dropper with a very solid pull. One of the fish took the dropper fly far down the tail under the alders on the far bank. I was lucky because I got two shots at that fish. It first surprised me with a swirl at the fast-moving fly – surprised me because I did not expect a take so far down the tail. I cast again and mended the line quickly, held the fly in the glide and, when the take came, it was very solid and definite. Both these fish were very lively and similar in size to what I had been catching throughout the week.

In retrospect, I suspect that, over Tuesday and Wednesday, despite our intended careful approach, the fish were becoming increasingly spooked. Thursday brought heavy rain and the river rose with a distinctly black stain. By Thursday evening, it had peaked on the two-foot mark and was starting to fall. I managed a lively three-pound sea trout that fell to a gaudy size-eight Cascade double.

By late Saturday afternoon, I was well resigned to accepting a total of eight grilse for the week. However, I tried the tail of a promising pool once more and got another take; this tail was proving to be a bit of a hot spot! The hook held and I was now on nine fish for the week. But I was also tired and, having fished through the upper pools, would have to traverse the jungle of the lower parts of the beat if I was to fish undisturbed water. Nine fish was good but ten fish would be tantalisingly better! I made the rough sojourn back to the car, travelled down the road and then scrambled once more down the steep brae to the lower pools. I had a choice: Turn right through the tall bracken and make the two river crossings necessary to access the upper and lower parts of a very good run or turn left through even taller and thicker bracken to access a lower pool that had not yielded anything all week. I decided on the upper option because it had given fish to me earlier in the week. However, it was all to no effect and, as the river became increasingly quiet, I sensed a possible change to the weather; there was a subtle closeness in the air that intimated the rainstorm that was to come later that evening. I waded back through the lower crossing and found myself at the riverside junction with the steep path that would take me back home. The alternative route provided the daunting prospect of yet another foray through the tangle that would lead eventually to the lower, less productive pool. I suppose there was always going to be a last cast – I had not performed the ritual of that scenario yet – so off I went! The pool looked good and I fished carefully through its length but, as with the pool above, to no effect. All that remained was the very tail under the alder stems of the far bank. I probably would not have bothered with this cast but for the fact that the extreme tails had proved so productive in other pools. So, this would be the last cast; not an easy one but one that could be rescued with a quick mend to steady the fly. The take was terrific – the best of the week – and the ensuing fight was spectacular! At one point, the fish made a very determined rush for the far bank upstream of where I stood. I could not stop it and it certainly waited until the very last instant before braking as it leapt under the branches of the far bank. It was a tremendous commotion that preceded one of the most spectacularly bizarre incidents that I have encountered in playing fish. It was now apparent that the fish had taken the dropper which could be seen clearly in its mouth; the tail fly was firmly embedded in the branch above its head! My line was taut and the fish was effectively suspended between the branch and my rod tip, with the weight of its body in the stream. I did not have much option in the matter, so trusting that the dropper fly (attached to the upper nylon) should hold fast, I pulled steadily for the break. To my relief, when this parody of a washing line 'snapped', the fish was still on. It continued to fight hard and fast before I could beach it at the tail of the pool. Strangely, the line had not in fact snapped; the tail fly had ripped free from the branch and my duo of Thunder Stoats was intact. This grilse was my only cock fish of the week, weighed five or six pounds and swam away strongly when released. It had a defiance which seemed to declare that any further efforts on my part would most definitely not be welcome. Time to go home!

I have written this account of rare success with scant reference to Les. We both encountered fish during the first three days but, as things turned out, these proved to be the only days that Les was on the river. On Wednesday night, he suffered a serious fall from which he has now, thankfully, recovered. As with most matters concerning Les, I think it better that he should recount the tale himself of how, on two successive years, he should have finished his week early and occupied a bed in the local hospital! I have known Les for a great many years and can assure you that he does not lack enthusiasm for his fishing. This is, after all, the man who used to cycle in the very early morning from St Monans in Fife to fish the Tay at Rome Croy in Perth. He has the distinction of arriving at first light to be first down the water and for the typical 'nailing' of fresh autumn fish for which the beat was renowned! How on earth he had the stamina and wherewithal to cycle home with the added burden of several heavy autumn fish is anyone's guess. In later years, he graduated to a motorcycle and eventually a car, which, by his own standards, must surely have verged on cheating. Whatever, through our shared joy of fishing and more, this thoughtful and caring man has become an increasingly close friend to whom I owe much. I have yet to meet a fisher – and I suspect I never shall – who is a more consistent catcher of salmon on the fly, be it on small or big rivers, in low or high water. Fishing our small river has meant fishing with Les and for that, I am a happy man. We shall return, although, in future years, I suspect our hosts Jim and Cathy may contact the hospital in advance to ensure that a bed is at the ready!

So, there we have it. I know a grand wee river that is well managed as a salmon fishery. It abounds with flora and fauna that bring joy to those with eyes to see and ears to listen. It is not always easy. In fact, it can be downright difficult to fish but, when it is 'on', my goodness, it is good! For me, it provides great motivation for endeavouring to keep physically fit and be of sound mind for as many years as possible.

A Final Cast

When I first started writing this book, I began with the 'Introduction'. I suspect that this is not always the order in which book chapters are written and that the content of an introduction or preface may often come last. I understand that, in some ways, it may be easier to write about what follows in the body of a book once the book has been written. However, in this instance, I had a pretty clear idea of what the subsequent chapter contents would be and, at the outset, the Introduction was easy writing. However, it was written a couple of years before the final chapters were completed and I now find that some of the sentiments and opinions expressed in the Introduction need some revision. I have opted to leave the Introduction as first written but to express some qualifying thoughts on its content in this final chapter.

I do not regret my sceptical stance on the current emphasis and assumed correctness of compulsory 'catch and release'. I love fishing but, unlike many who currently write on the subject, I do like to have the option of keeping the occasional fish, including Atlantic salmon. In my writings, I hope that I have made it clear that I am no butcher of fish. I marvel at pictures from the not-so-distant past of rod-caught salmon arrayed outside some fishing hut. These catches were phenomenal but they relate to times when wild fish were plentiful and sold as an accepted means whereby tenants paid for a fishing week. It is now illegal (and undesirable) to catch and sell rod-caught salmon in this manner. Let it be clear, I have no stomach for such indiscriminate killing of large numbers of fish as was formerly practised. I am glad that I was never part of that scene and I hope such practice remains firmly in the past. However, such wholesale slaughter is very different from the keeping of an occasional fish. For me, the implications of a policy whereby the occasional fish might be kept at the discretion of an angler, as opposed to an outright ban on the killing of fish, are profound. I stated so in the Introduction to this book where I was at pains to make clear my position in this regard.

I have not changed my stance on this matter. However, what has changed is the extent to which catch and release has been adopted as mandatory or accepted policy on different rivers and beats throughout Scotland. It is now a much more wide-spread phenomenon than was previously the case and has assumed something like majority practice on most rivers during most (and often all) of the season. Initially the emphasis was on conserving spring stocks following the alarming decline in spring runs. It has now spread on many rivers to encompass most of the season with occasional, selective exceptions regarding autumn-run fish. So, I am now confronted with a situation on the rivers I mostly fish, where the retention of any fish would now contravene Government decree, local agreement or, at best, what is deemed to be acceptable behaviour on the beats I fish. In the Introduction, I stated that where the compulsory release of spring salmon is a requirement, you would no longer find me on the water. I also stated that my friends had come to accept this stance. My dilemma is, of course, that this stance should now mostly prevail for the whole season and on most rivers, meaning that salmon fishing, for me, should be a thing of the past. But this is not the case and there are several reasons why this should be so. The first is somewhat spurious and I take no great pleasure in its rationale, mostly because I cannot justify my stance. At worst, it is an admission of downright weakness and insincerity; at best, it is an admission of addiction. Perhaps I should give up fishing for salmon completely. If the stock is so much at risk of extinction, then perhaps we should all refrain from fishing. But I want to fish. More than that, I find it extremely difficult and very much diminishing to my very being not to fish. There we have it: The confession of an addict. I have a sneaking suspicion that, come what may, I shall always be found with a rod in hand. Many will understand this state; others who are not smitten will find it incomprehensible. So, where I once was reluctant to fish during the restrictions of the spring season, I shall now do so with equal integrity (or lack of it) as I do at any other time of year.

The whole question of compulsory catch and release needs serious critique both on grounds of honesty and pragmatism. In recent seasons, I have too often been witness to the return of dying or dead fish to the river by anglers who are complying with expectation. I am not critical of the actual rod that has hooked, played fairly and then returned quickly a hard-earned fish that is subsequently dead or dies on release. Such anglers are respecting the terms as stipulated on their permit and they are potentially in serious trouble if found to be doing otherwise. My problem lies with the lack of sense in the legislative matter. It might be argued that most migratory fish in the river will eventually die anyway, so the returning of a dead or dying fish is only accelerating the inevitable. But would the retention of one or two weakened or dead fish on the part of anglers be of any real consequence to the bigger picture of salmon conservation? I doubt if that is the case and, in the overall scheme of things, it seems salutary to remember that most if not all stipulations on the release of rod-caught salmon are now made in the name of conservation. Incredible as it might seem to those who fished in a bygone age, I and many others have frequently witnessed the return of salmon in recent seasons that are already dead or have very little chance of survival. Sometimes (but not always) these are fish caught by inexperienced rods. This is hardly the fault of the rods themselves; it is just that they have not had much opportunity or experience in the playing, landing and handling of salmon. What is less acceptable (to me at any rate) is the apparent burgeoning necessity to get pictorial evidence of fish caught. As far as I am aware, this is a self-imposed practice as opposed to something requested by any fishery. Regrettably, I have seen this 'paparazzi' syndrome quite literally result in fish being photographed to death before being returned to the water. I understand the attraction of having an image of the catch, perhaps especially so if it is to be released. But is this practice necessary? Must we have a picture to enjoy – and even to relive – the thrill of the moment? For my part, I find the reading of a story or listening to a play on the radio to be just as engaging as watching a film of the same event. Is there a lesson to be learnt here? God knows – and I am sure my long-suffering family will agree – I have photographed hundreds of fish but these were fish that I had already killed by design as opposed to killing inadvertently by the inevitable delay in getting a pictorial record.

I mentioned the issue of honesty pertaining to catch and release. No doubt there are many authorities and individuals who are scrupulously consistent in their observance of this policy but it is not always so. Lack of adherence to stated policy at best smacks of weakness and at worst is downright deceitful and hypocritical. If you have the jurisdiction to do otherwise, why pay lip service to some policy with which you disagree? It all smacks of poor resolve to challenge an insidious political correctness. I know of one beat that, for many years, has had a very stringent and clearly stated policy in support of catch and release. On a recent visit, I was utterly amazed to find the fishing hut newly equipped with weighing scales, cleaning sink and chest freezer. Make what you will of that!

For all that I have admitted to the addictive nature of fishing that now sees me, as never previously, on waters with a policy of compulsory catch and release, there is at least one other compelling reason why I continue to fish. Recently, Scottish anglers had the opportunity of commenting on proposed legislation pertaining to rod fishing for salmon in Scottish rivers. In my view, the Government consultation paper was well written. I know of many good and well-stated responses to the proposals and I like to think that the efforts of respondents may have had some bearing on the current legislation. One of the great things about this whole exercise was that it got people thinking clearly about how they saw the future of Scottish salmon fishing. For my own part, where I once had some vague and largely unstated notions on what I considered meaningful, I now have a much more clearly stated conviction regarding the way ahead. The matter is not simple but some key points are worth noting. As stated earlier, the declared driver for the current burst of legislation is the conservation of the Atlantic salmon. Now, although this may seem a laudable intention, it is arguably a motive that at best is tenuous and at worst so poorly defined that meaningful policy for its implementation cannot be formulated. At one level, conservation of a species might imply the sustained recruitment of individuals to replace mortality such that the species would survive. In the case of the Atlantic salmon, it may well be that surprisingly few adult fish, returning safely to their home rivers, might result in sufficient progeny for the species to survive. However, from an angling point of view, this base-line population for survival may be grossly inadequate. Anglers need to be fishing a stock that well exceeds the minimum requirement for species survival.

So, why bother with anglers and their predatory intervention on the salmon stock? Why indeed! Well, the answer to this reasonable question is not trivial. Conservation as a notion is all very well but, at least in the public domain, it is very often portrayed in a very piecemeal manner. Salmon are, of course, part of a much bigger ecosystem, where intervention in favour of any one species is likely to impact on others. The system can be tremendously complex in terms of species interaction and system behaviour. In recent decades, there have been legislative efforts apparently favouring the conservation of target species. In river systems and coastal waters, these have resulted in enhanced populations of bird species such as sawbills (including shags, cormorants, mergansers and goosanders), sea mammals such as seals, porpoises and dolphins and river mammals such as otters. As it so happens I, and I suspect most anglers, have a keen interest in the welfare of all these species. What causes me considerable alarm is the unfounded effort at enhancing populations of some of these species in an uninformed and biased manner. For decades, the regulation of seal and dolphin numbers has been considered unacceptable in the public eye; in like manner, the regulation of sawbill numbers. But do we seriously consider it natural and indeed desirable that seals and cormorants should be found regularly well upstream of estuarial waters, well away from what we understand to be their normal coastal habitats? They are obviously feeding on something and it seems likely that some or all stages in the life cycle of Atlantic salmon will be food targets. So, here we have it: Popular opinion (not strictly from the point of view of ecosystem conservation) is favouring populations of some species at the expense of others, such as the Atlantic salmon. The issue is further clouded by recreational interests (previously, solely the angling fraternity). It is now a well-advertised and popular pastime to go dolphin watching at the mouth of the Aberdeenshire Dee – a river that has, in recent years, suffered massive declines in salmon runs. All good and well but do we truly want to encourage seal and dolphin numbers at the expense of endangered salmon stocks? The issue is lacking in anything approaching joined-up thinking.

For a sustainable ecosystem, we require a stated intention of population numbers and species demography, not just of one species but ideally of all species or functional groups that we understand to be important in the food chain and behavioural interactions. But this does not mean that all species should be represented by populations that are essentially base-line to their respective survival. It is quite in order that, in a managed system, population targets should be set that might favour numbers of some species over others, without detracting from the sustainability of the whole system and its component species. How do we identify such target species whose numbers might be favoured? I think this is where we come to the crux of the matter. Whatever our targets, some form of monitoring is required if we are to have any sense of stability or change in the system. Moreover, we most certainly require some form of policing of the whole venture to ensure that overall conservation interests are being met. For years, the one body of people who have consistently patrolled the riverbanks in a voluntary and conscientious manner has been that of the angling fraternity. There will always be exceptions, but most anglers have the interests of all riverside flora and fauna at heart. I would go as far as saying that anglers have been, and continue to be, the unsung, unrecognised conservationists of the river system.

They are mostly natural historians with a very keen interest in the overall welfare of the river. They marvel at the behaviour of seals and dolphins but they do not wish to see them impacting negatively in an unregulated manner on fish stocks. This attitude prevails for all predators of fish. It is not the predators as such that cause grief and ill feeling within the angling body but the unregulated numbers of predators when fish stocks are so threatened as is currently the case.

There is an anomaly here. If anglers truly are the real conservationists, then their voice has often gone unheard. Membership in angling clubs up and down the land is fragile and the angling body has been an easy target for desperate measures at protecting dwindling fish stocks – hence the authoritarian approval of catch and release. This is a pretty absurd position given that, in the Government's own consultation document, they made clear that most fish caught by anglers were being returned to the water anyway! There is a very strong argument that, in the interests of ecosystem conservation, the angling body should thrive. It is anglers up and down the banks of rivers that report on instances of pollution and that make observations on flora and fauna and communicate this information on request. Their presence ensures that riverbanks are patrolled and that unacceptable practices are minimised – not just in the immediate context of catching fish but in most areas of conservation, such as the regulation of invasive species of plants and animals. Anglers do this because the want to; they are mostly enthusiasts for the natural environment. And, most wonderfully, they do this free of charge. They even pay for the privilege of doing this when purchasing their fishing permit! Is it asking too much that the angling body might be free of petty restriction and find enhanced enthusiasm for their efforts? Might not the keeping of an occasional fish from a population that exceeds the base-line requirement for species survival constitute a reasonable expectation? Remember, that it is this very option that motivates so many anglers, the thing that makes the whole venture meaningful! The keeping of occasional dead or dying fish might be a very good start to ensuring the continued presence of these unsung conservationists on the riverbank. Who else is going to do the job? We do not have the resources to fund the necessary bailiffs and, in all honesty, I doubt if many of them would have the overall expertise and enthusiasm of the typical angler for the whole ecosystem.

So, there you have it. I am advocating the angling body as being the conservation body par excellence. There will always be exceptions to the rule but, in my experience, the angling body is self-regulating; miscreants are generally made very unwelcome on the riverbanks. Anglers are the true natural historians of their environment, taking a keen interest in the welfare of all species. They pay for the privilege of being on the riverbank. Their prime concern is the catching of fish and, in this regard, any petty intervention to the occasional keeping of fish is unnecessary; most fish are now returned anyway. We should ensure that populations of fish predators are not so high as to allow for a small surplus of fish that might be caught and kept. With this hope in mind, I shall continue to fish for salmon. I hope my presence and voice will contribute to the sustainability of the river in its entirety.

I wrote earlier of my enthusiasm for being on the water and how the very anticipation of a fishing trip was an integral and very important part of the venture. This remains true but my position is somewhat ambivalent. This summer (at the time of writing) will find Doug, Les and me on the banks of a massive push of water in the north of Sweden. We share an excitement at the prospect. Doug, of course, has a plethora of flies already tied for the job, all beautiful creations. I am sure he will tie more. Les will have tied his usual stuff with some possible nod towards enhanced visual impact. I suppose, I shall get around to tying something sometime. The flights and accommodation are booked and we continue to avidly read about the place and peruse video clips. It all looks tremendous! I hope and expect that my companions will catch fish. I would love to feel the weight of one of the heavy brigade for which this water is renowned. It must be an incredible experience to have one of these monsters pull and then run line in the tumultuous flow of this arctic water. We have nothing like it in Scotland; the lower reaches of the Tay in full (but unfishable) flood would be our closest match. Whatever happens, I shall enjoy this trip, even if the solid draw of a fish be denied me. And here lies the ambivalence: My enthusiasm for the effort remains undaunted but my concern over the actual catching of fish has diminished.

At face value, this ambivalence may be a cause for concern but, strangely, I do not find this to be the case. I still love moments of success in terms of fish numbers and size. However, blank days are a common feature of today's salmon fishing and, thankfully, I now find that I can take them in my stride, perhaps with better grace than previously. I have so many clear and fond memories of fishing that I need only shut my eyes and dream to savour the fullness of the moment. The chronology of memory is unimportant. I get as much thrill reliving the early capture of a Craggie trout as the more recent capture of an Esk grilse. The capture of a Swedish leviathan will add to the memories but its absence will be of little consequence. I find this sentiment reassuring because my days on the water will no doubt become progressively compromised as old age and infirmity consume me. I would like to think that I might have another ten or so good years by loch and stream but who knows what might befall me? The joy is that, come what may, I have the memories. I now know that I shall get as much pleasure out of watching others fish, reading about fishing or reflecting on my earlier escapades, as I currently do in my actual fishing. There is something wonderfully comforting in this!

I do not wish to be morose on the matter of age but I do seek to find my place in the scheme of things. Many of those who meant so much to me throughout my fishing years have passed away. They remain my friends. My affection for dear, irascible Sandy who so generously left me part of his fishing legacy when I was so young and ignorant is strong; I wish I had thanked him properly in later years. I wish I could meet again the man from Stow whose ten-minute tutorial on the banks of the Gala was so important but he too will be long-gone. I rejoice in the affection of Maggie-Anne and Alec towards me in my young years. In my mind, I can still see and hear them clearly as their smiles and lilting voices caress me on some light and sunny morning. More recently, my early mentor, Bill Currie, was laid to rest. I did not know the man beyond his books (although I met him when I was young) but he was important to me. In like manner, I noted the recent passing of Bruce Sandison with regret but also gratitude for the way in which he enticed me to explore so many trout lochs, not least Craggie. And, for me, Craggie has also changed with the recent passing of David Walker from whom I rented the fishing and of Margaret at the caravan park; they were both such integral parts of my Craggie experience.

I am aware that people have become increasingly important to my appreciation of fishing; the passing of so many has made me reflect on this matter. I have dedicated this book to Les, Dennis, Vic and Doug because they are the fishing companions to whom I owe most. They all bear the stamp of uncompromising generosity and I have told of this in my writings. Les has been there more or less from the start. (Okay, so there was a gap of more than thirty years when I had not the faintest idea what he was doing!) He is an integral part of my fishing and, therefore, my life. He is a truly great friend with whom I share most things, not least the deeper things (including fishing) of life. He has opened my eyes to much of what I know of angling literature and for this, I am most grateful. I think some of the most evocative writing in the English language must pertain to fishing and Les has read and shared with me a great part of this heritage. In recent years, I often met with Dennis and it has been a joy to chat and laugh at shared memories. It was Dennis who got me going seriously on my salmon fishing. Vic remains a close friend. I would not have had any of my fishing on the South and North Esks had it not been for him. At the time of writing, Vic has just retired and I look forward to sharing much more fishing time with him. Doug? Well, Doug is just Doug, known to one and all as the most helpful of people in matters to do with fishing and beyond. He has become a wonderful companion on the riverbank and beyond. There are many more whom I have befriended on the river but it is to these four that I owe so much.

I close these writings by stating that, quite incongruously, I am seated in the afternoon shade of a scorching Australian summer day. Eilidh moved to Melbourne years ago and it is a joy to visit and be surrounded by energetic grandchildren whilst enjoying the unbridled hospitality of my son-in-law. They help keep me young! It is now the latter half of January and Doug has already made three outings to the Tay during the first week of the salmon season. He assures me it is like a balmy March day in Perthshire. My goodness he is keen! Whatever else, he will be honing his skills in preparation for the visit to Sweden. I suspect Les will be having a slightly more leisurely start to his season but shortly he too will be found on the banks of Tay and Tummel. In a few weeks' time, I shall venture forth with Doug, Les and Vic on the banks of South or North Esk and another season will have started for us all.

This time of relaxation with my grandchildren has prompted me to dwell on the whole matter of inheritance. Dennis astounded Doug and me by passing on much of his fishing tackle to us. I recall a regular rod at Kercock doing the same for Dennis at the end of a day's fishing. The man knew he would not be using his tackle again and wanted Dennis to have it. It was a poignant moment. My time will come for doing likewise. When that time arrives, I would like to think that my gear will go to someone who sees some intrinsic value in its content and heritage. But, of course, a lot of it will be outmoded. Most of my friends would not countenance using the big heavy double-handers that I wield for salmon in bigger waters. I love their action and see no reason to change my habits. A lot of what I inherited from Sandy was way past its best at the time but the thing is it got me started. What remains as evidence of Sandy's generosity to me is now much treasured.

I have been fishing (thanks to Doug) with my eldest grandson Euan. We caught some lovely rainbows and I guess he was thrilled. However, which, if any, of my grandchildren will become truly smitten by the fishing obsession remains to be seen. Klara is particularly keen (loves casting) and both she and Mårten show real determination to persevere, even when fish are not being caught – always a good sign! Susanna loves water and stones and has been fishing enthusiastically with David and myself. Michael is good at anything physical that requires timing and the whole business of casting will come easily to him. And now we have Sandy. There would be something poignantly complete if Sandy was to enthuse about fishing as did his long-past namesake from whom I inherited my early tackle. However, it is quite possible that none of my grandchildren will follow in my footsteps when it comes to fishing and, if that be the case, I shall rest easy – fishing is not for everyone! On the other hand, perhaps for one or more of them, my writings and apparent enthusiasm for the whole business will be the addictive spark of a lifetime. Time will tell!